Advance Praise for
Working Together: Producing Synergy by Honoring Diversity

"The marvelous anthology before you literally swells with insight and wisdom as some of today's top minds come together in the common cause of unity and hope—that a world so diverse can learn to truly value and embrace it's differences."
—Stephen R. Covey, author,
The Seven Habits of Highly Effective People

"*Working Together: Producing Synergy by Honoring Diversity* adds greatly to our understanding of the complexities of diversity."
—Isabel O. Lopez, president
Lopez Leadership Services

"*Working Together*—a truly timely, inspirational book by a striking line-up of writers."
—Max DePree, author

"*Working Together* offers wise insights into building enriched, inclusive communities within the workplace and beyond."
—Ann DeBusk, executive director
American Leadership Forum, Silicon Valley

"*Working Together* raises a key issue for our times with unusual depth and insight."
—Thomas Moore, author
Care of the Soul and
The Re-Enchantment of Everyday Life

"Any system (body, computer, chair, etc.) only works because its parts are different and relate to one another. Accordingly, any organization or team or partnership is only as functional as the degree to which its members relate effectively across differences to meet common objectives. *Working Together* has created synergy by honoring its own diversity, resulting in total impact even greater than the sum of its excellent parts."

Diversity," "No

"This is an outstanding collection of authors/articles that are inspirational and practical. It provides keen insights into how we can best produce the synergy of working together by respecting and working with the diversity in our workforce, our organizations, and our lives."
>—Davis C. Wiggelsworth, PhD, president
>D.C.W. Research Associates International

"A superb collection of profound learnings about bridging differences and making a difference. The personal experience and insight reflected in these chapters taps the values, spirit and responsibility inherent in diversity and provides timely, inspiring perspectives on living and working together in the 21st Century global village."
>—David W. Jamieson, co-author,
>*Managing Workforce 2000*

"Reading this book is like stringing together a beautiful necklace where each person's story adds a multifaceted and unique jewel of insight. The string that connects these essays is an elegant consistency for such values as awareness, vulnerability, learning, and inclusion braided together with suggestions and methods for respectfully finding common ground while inviting and cherishing difference."
>—Barbara Shipka, author,
>*Leadership in a Challenging World*

"In *Working Together,* New Leaders Press effectively presents the principles and strategies that will help to develop the inclusive workplace of the future."
>—David Jamison
>Jamison Cawdry Advertising

"This book helps illuminate the complex and sometimes puzzling idea of diversity by presenting a range of perspectives demonstrating that there are many approaches to diversity. A reader will leave this book challenged and enlightened."
>—Lawrence Perlman, chairman and CEO
>Ceridian Corporation

"This anthology is an excellent chronicle of how diversity will impact the global community into the 21st Century."
>—William A. Guillory, president and CEO
>Innovations International, Inc.

WORKING TOGETHER
Diversity as Opportunity

Angeles Arrien, Editor

Featuring writings by:

Mikhail Gorbachev • Riane Eisler • Norman Lear
Gary Janka • Dianne Campton • Wendy Luhabe
Marilyn Hill Harper and Wendy S. Appel • Suzie Williams
Michael Welp • David Goff • Perviz Randeria
Patrick O'Neill • Jacqueline Haessly • Sylvia Lafair
BJ Gallagher Hateley and Warren H. Schmidt
Joy Carver • James Calvin • John O'Neil

BK

BERRETT-KOEHLER PUBLISHERS, INC.
San Francisco

Berrett-Koehler Publishers, Inc.
450 Sansome Street, Suite 1200
San Francisco, CA 94111-3320
Tel: (415) 288-0260
Fax: (415) 362-2512
www.bkconnection.com

ORDERING INFORMATION
Quantity sales. Special discounts are available on quantity purchases by corporations, associations, and others. For details, contact the "Special Sales Department" at the Berrett-Koehler address above.

Individual sales. Berrett-Koehler publications are available through most bookstores. They can also be ordered direct from Berrett-Koehler: Tel: (800) 929-2929; Fax: (802) 864-7626; www.bkconnection.com.

Orders for college textbook/course adoption use. Please contact Berrett-Koehler: Tel: (800) 929-2929; Fax: (802) 864-7626.

Orders by U.S. trade bookstores and wholesalers. Please contact Publishers Group West, 1700 Fourth Street, Berkeley, CA 94710.
Tel: (510) 528-1444; Fax (510) 528-3444.

Permissions and Credits
The editor and publisher wish to acknowledge the following sources:

The Gorbachev Foundation and Pavel Palazchenko for their permission to reprint Mikhail Gorbachev's writings, excerpted from his book, The Search for a New Beginning: Developing a New Civilization.

The Institute of Noetic Sciences for their permission to reprint Norman Lear's essay, previously published in their Review, a quarterly journal.

Photo credits:
Riane Eisler: page 18, Shumel Thaler
Norman Lear: page 118: Linda Solomon.

Printed in the United States of America.
Printed on acid-free and recycled paper that is composed of 80% recovered fiber, including 30% post consumer waste).

Library of Congress Cataloging-in-Publication Data
Working together: diversity as opportunity / Angeles Arrien, editor; featuring writings by
Mikhail Gorbachev ...[et al.]
   p.cm.
   Originally published: Pleasanton, CA: New Leaders Press; Lanham, MD: National Book
Network [distributor[, c1998. Reissued 2001 with editorial changes.
   Includes bibliographical references and index.
   ISBN 1-57675-156-2 ✓
   1. Diversity in the workplace. 2. Multiculturalism. 3. Interpersonal relations.   I. Arrien,
Angeles, 1940– . II. Gorbachev, Mikhail Sergeevich, 1931– .
HF5549.5.M5W672 2001
331.11--dc21
                                                                2001025161

First Edition
06   05   04   03   02   01   10 9   8   7   6   5   4   3   2   1
Typography by Select Press.

Table of Contents

Preface

Cultural diversity is a business reality today. The ability to build bridges between people from different countries, with different ethnic backgrounds, is as important as any other business function. Working in a culturally and ethically diverse organization does not mean eliminating differences in styles and approach, but celebrating those differences and tapping into the many strengths that diversity brings to an organization.

This anthology is a collection of articles that looks at diversity as an opportunity rather than a problem to be solved. Each article either conceptually or practically offers a perspective or learning that fosters respect for and appreciation of differences, and demonstrates how the practice of this theme alone clearly increases and helps teamwork productivity and morale within organizations, communities, and families.

There have been many books about diversity over the years, many of which focused on the workplace. This book attempts to deal with mindsets and core beliefs—the origins of difficulties and resistance to diversity. It is a context-setter for a true "mind-change"—from seeing diversity as only associated with affirmative actions, racial issues, and difficult differences, to seeing diversity as a rich creative resource to be utilized.

If we can see diversity as a rich resource that holds multiples of promise for unimaginable outcomes, then perhaps we can have the change of consciousness that Mikhail Gorbachev means when he writes, "having changed ourselves, we must come together in all our diversity to build a New World." How can we use the social koan of diversity to facilitate self-development, cultural change, and global interdependence? It seems that we face a dilemma. In order to get along with the business of human existence we must learn how to get along with each other. As we stand crowded together at this important evolutionary threshold, we must discover how to collaborate without the righteous insistence about particular outcomes that inevitably threaten other's survival. Becoming responsible for a whole larger than ourselves, we must learn how to retain our own integrity without insisting that others forsake their integrity. Most important, it helps to realize that the underlying struggle for our future is not between conservatives and liberals, or between science and religion; but, as Riane Eisler points out, between a *dominator paradigm*, that automatically ranks humanity into those on top and those on the bottom, and a *partnership paradigm* where valuing difference can be the basis for a less tense and more interesting and creative way of living and working. It will take time to change entrenched patterns of belief and behavior. We can accelerate that process by playing a conscious and active part in constructing the foundations for a workplace—and a world where diversity can be truly honored.

Norman Lear reminds us that the great challenge of our time is to live up to one of our nation's founding credos, *E Pluribus Unum: out of many, one.* But the feeling of unity without conformity almost certainly will not emerge from politics or economics as we know them today. If we are truly to respect and honor one another as members of one human family, we must begin to draw up some new mental maps for a new century and beyond—maps that begin to sketch out the lost continent of the human spirit: the capacity for awe, wonder, mystery, art, music, love, compassion, and the search for higher meaning.

Perhaps this internal human drive for meaning is a force which will galvanize an evolutionary acceleration for the human spirit to recognize that the opportunity of WORKING TOGETHER is in service of something greater, *something mysterious* that will ultimately transform self and society within multiple learning crucibles called diversity. Our challenge is to open to the mystery of what can be created when two or more join to create a greater good for all concerned.

It is the hope of the editor and the nineteen authors included within this book that the greater service diversity provides is a consciousness raising opportunity that can foster collaboration, cooperation, and mutual respect. Where we dare to dream and creatively problem solve together, is where we can co-create what Gorbachev calls, "a civilization of mutual tolerance with cultures and nations becoming increasingly open minded and where diversity is understood and used as a factor of progress."

This may be the creative enterprise that will propel the human spirit to move forward a collaborative commitment to engage in a civilization that assures creative co-existence, mutual preservation, and common values that sustain and enhance humanity and nature as a whole. This is the opportunity, blessing, and challenge of our time. May we join to create a world that works for everyone. It is diversity's opportunity.

— Angeles Arrien
Sausalito, CA

Acknowledgments

This book has been a true collaboration involving far more people than those listed as authors or co-authors of this anthology. There are those who were key supporters to the contributors, those who helped produce and design the book, and many others "behind the scenes" who should be acknowledged.

Starting with authors, David Goff especially wishes to acknowledge Cynthia McReynolds, co-founder of A Foundation for Interdependence. She first identified the paradox associated with building community through diversity as a "social koan" and should rightfully be considered a co-author of this article. The underlying insights that inform this article also represent the cumulative voices of many participants in a variety of learning communities. He wishes to thank those many others who, facing themselves, each other, and the mystery of human existence, made palpable how radically interconnected we are with each other and the larger process of nature. He also wishes to extend a special thanks to those trailblazers who are showing the way to this ambiguous and paradoxical reality: the late Victor Turner, Scott Peck, The Foundation for Community Encouragement, Joanna R. Macy, Arnold Mindell, and Angeles Arrien.

Wendy Nomathemba Luhabe is grateful to Princess Molefe who typed the manuscript with very few mistakes, putting up with her endless changes and rearranging; to Khosi Jiyane who offered her immaculate expertise to ensure she would be understood; to Roy Cardy who indulged her in a week away from the business so she could put her thoughts on paper; and to all her valuable clients for their support and partnership—particularly Nick Dennis at Tiger Oats. "Nangomso Angeles Arrien, Warrior Woman!"

Suzie Williams would like to express her gratitude with the following words: Every person who has touched my life has helped shape it. It would take a separate book to publicly acknowledge all the beautiful souls who have had a profound affect on me. Many of you recognize the importance you play in my life. Many of you have touched my life and have no idea the gifts you have given me. To each of you, I send love and a debt of gratitude.

Michael Welp wishes to acknowledge his partner, Kim Marshall, and two mentors at the Fielding Institute, Charlie Seashore and the late Leonard Hirsch for believing in him and nurturing his growth. Thanks and best wishes go to Class 18 of the American University/NTL Institute Masters Program in OD and to the Outward Bound School of Lesotho in Southern Africa. Thanks to many friends, colleagues and teachers who have contributed to his learning in the area of diversity.

Perviz E. Randeria would like to dedicate her article to her parents, Edulji and Banoo Randeria, as they were very special people who were wonderful examples of living one's values.

She would also like to acknowledge Angeles Arrien as a gifted teacher and an inspiring guide to "walking the spiritual path with practical feet." She is grateful for Arrien's invitation and encouragement in writing for this anthology. She also wishes to thank Maurice Monette for his editing work. She appreciates his focus, clarity, and crispness while retaining the essence of her writing.

Patrick O'Neill wishes to dedicate his essay to the memory of his mother, Mildred Evelyn O'Neill.

Jacqueline Haessly wishes to acknowledge her daughter Kris, and her sons: Fran, Randy, Ernie, and Mike, whose rainbow hue allows her to experience diversity in rich ways within her own family, and her husband Dan Di Domizio, for welcoming this rainbow mix into his life, and her mother for starting it all. She also wants to acknowledge the thousands of people—educators, parents, students, and friends—who have participated in one or more of the thousands of Respect for Diversity workshops over the past twenty-eight years. Finally, she wants to acknowledge those scholars whose work had enriched her own thinking: Clarence Williams, bell hooks, Pat Mische, Chandra Talpade Mohanty, Harriet Alonso, Elizabeth Minnich, Robert Muller, and Patricia Williams. Each has deepened her awareness of what it means to live joyfully in a richly diverse world.

Joy Carver thanks the Lord for all of her gifts and talents, and her two sons Tom and Dion for their love, patience, and forgiveness during her absences as she sought to reach out to the global community to teach, learn, and grow as a human being.

Angeles Arrien, the book's editor, wishes to acknowledge each of the contributing authors for their pioneering efforts, creative and practical skills, and committed vision to honoring diversity to produce synergistic results. The book itself stands as an example of what happens when many diverse gifts, talents, and perspectives come together to create something greater than any of its parts. From Angeles's point of view, this anthology could not have come into being without the excellent stewardship, coaching, and consistent support that John Renesch provided to the editor and all the authors throughout the process of *working together* in creating the original hardcover edition of this book. John's leadership and vision will always remain a source of inspiration to her. She is deeply grateful to John for extending this opportunity to her. To Claudette Allison of New Leaders Press, Angeles extends respect for her consistent focus, flexibility, support, and follow-through. To her own staff, Angeles could not have pulled this anthology together without her executive administrator, Victoria Engel, and her production administrator, Patricia Rockwell. To both of them, she is grateful for the unlimited support they provided to her as needed. Finally, Angeles acknowledges her Basque heritage and ancestors for providing the cultural conditioning and modeling for economic self-sufficiency by *working together*. Her hope is that this book will provide a rich legacy to all generations of the future and be a practical and inspirational resource for anyone working with diversity issues, personally or professionally.

The creators of this collection thank everyone associated with this project, most prominently all the contributing authors, knowing that coordinating the efforts of so many people requires much cooperation and organizational focus as well as the talent for expression. In addition, thanks go to the book's editor Angeles Arrien, John Renesch, and former New Leaders Press staff members Claudette Allison, Darcy Brown, and Tatiana Roegiers for their direct involvement. Deep appreciation also goes out to the production and design people, namely Carolynn Crandall and Karen Deist and their team at Select Press for typography, and Sue Malikowski of Autographics for her artwork and cover. Renesch offers a special thanks to Jacqueline Haessly and Barbara Shipka for their probing and prodding him over recent years about a book on this topic. He also wishes to give profound thanks to Angeles Arrien, his partner in this book, who made the vision real after it had lived only as an idea for three years.

For their roles in negotiating the whitewater of copyrights and legalities, we acknowledge the Institute of Noetic Sciences, and the Gorbachev Foundation, including the gracious Pavel Palazchenko of Moscow.

Finally, on behalf of everyone connected with this book, the creators of this collection send a special "thank you" to those who took the time to preview this book in its earlier format as a hardcover book." These people are Ann DeBusk, Max DePree, Stephen R. Covey, Lewis Brown Griggs, William A. Guillory, David W. Jamieson, David Jamison, Isabel O. Lopez, Thomas Moore, Lawrence Perlman, Barbara Shipka, and Davis C. Wiggelsworth. Finally, we are all grateful and excited to have Berrett-Koehler Publishers as our new publisher and we thank Steve Piersanti and his diverse and collaborative team. We are honored to be part of Berrett-Koehler's highly-regarded book list and look forward to this cooperative effort.

"The World does not stay attached to a particular invention. It seeks diversity. It wants to move on to more inventing, to more possibilities. The world's desire for diversity compels us to change."

—from *A Simpler Way*
by Margaret J. Wheatley
and Myron Kellner-Rogers

Angeles Arrien is an anthropologist, educator, award-winning author, and corporate consultant. She lectures nationally and internationally, and conducts workshops that bridge cultural anthropology, psychology, and mediation skills. She teaches the universal components of communication, leadership skills, education, and health care. Her work reveals how indigenous wisdoms are relevant in our families, professional lives, and our relationship with our environment. She is president and founder of the Foundation for Cross-Cultural Education and Research, and a Fellow at the Institute of Noetic Sciences.

Arrien is the author of *The Four Fold Way: Walking the Paths of the Warrior, Teacher, Healer, and Visionary*, and *Signs of Life: The Five Universal Shapes and How to Use Them* (winner of the 1993 Benjamin Franklin Award).

Introduction

Angeles Arrien

> "The beauty and uniqueness of life lies in the unity of diversity."
>
> —Mikhail Gorbachev

What are the ways that we can benefit from the creative potency that diversity offers today? How can we create openings to foster different decision-making processes and communication skills so we can develop enough common ground and mutual acceptance to collaboratively work together and complete a task? This anthology is an attempt to bring together methods, skills, stories, and resources that foster collaboration and synergetic results for the common good of all concerned. It is, by no means, complete or representational of all the multicultural and subcultural issues and viewpoints. Rather, the articles have been selected for practical and broadening purposes and ways that we can touch the human spirit, to respect diversity, and to welcome the creativity and myriad results that multiculturalism and interdependence offer.

Diversity is known by many different names—pluralism, unity, harmony, tolerance, inclusion, conflict mediation, facilitation, equity, intercultural understanding, antibias, multicultural education, equal employment opportunity, affirmative action, cultural competence, global competitiveness, social justice, racial understanding, and being politically correct. All these terms reveal a need to relate, communicate, and work from a deeper place of respect, honor, integrity, heart, and wisdom. How do we do this? Kate Ludeman, PhD, in her book *The Worth Ethic*, provides a series of reminders and a collection of relevant research that may provide markers of where we may need to refocus our attention in order to support multicultural and intergenerational peoples working together synergistically. Here are four important trends that I see shaping us at this time— trends that signal ways to work together more effectively and productively.

Trend 1: A High Need for Communication and People Skills

- The Bureau of Vocational Guidance at Harvard, found that at least two-thirds of the people who lose their jobs do not do so because they cannot do the work, but because of their inability to deal effectively with people.

- The Center for Creative Leadership in Greensboro, North Carolina, shows that most fired executives are poor communicators.

- The National Alliance of Business warns that "...an uneducated work force is an unmotivated and unproductive one."

- Freelance writer Joanne Selement, with Kate Ludeman, asked top executives from 25 successful high-growth Silicon Valley companies to account for the most abrupt leaps they made in their careers. One-third said moves to challenging new jobs supercharged their careers; one-third cited formal training programs that improved their leadership behavior; and one-third described the importance of a mentor or coach who gave them regular feedback and took an active role in their development.

- When the Carnegie Institute of Technology analyzed the records of 10,000 people, it concluded that 15 percent of success comes from technical skill on the job and 85 percent from the ability to deal with people successfully.

- It is safe to assume that problems encountered at work are mostly communicative, not substantiative.

- A study by the White House Office of Consumer Affairs shows that 96% of unhappy customers never complained to the stores where they received poor service or goods, but *91percent won't buy again from the same place* and, on average, *they will share their bad experience with nine other people.*

- The most necessary skill needed, besides computer competence, may be listening and relating skills.

Trend 2: Importance and Impact of Integrity, Enjoyment, and Self-esteem

- Will Schutz, San Francisco psychologist and business consultant, says that if *people in companies told the truth, 80% to 90% of their problems would disappear.* When we act with honor, we discover that people are "relentlessly reasonable, cooperative, and capable of coming to sensible and productive agreements when they are dealt with directly."

- The work force in the 21st Century faces three obstacles to success in adopting and supporting ethics that align with integrity: (a) substituting manipulation for real change, (b) lacking discipline and dedication to your efforts, and (c) failing to deal with potential resentment. In *Management,* Peter Drucker warns that controlling and manipulating or strategizing without direct communication is a "...self-destructive abuse of knowledge." Ultimately, we hurt ourselves as well as our colleagues and employees when we say the right words and use the right techniques without matching them to honest feelings and intentions.

- Research by management consultant Harry Levinson, previously a business professor at Harvard University, shows successful CEOs can accurately assess their effectiveness as leaders, but many managers who fail to make it to the CEO level lack this ability; still, they are afraid to ask for advice. They fear that a confidante will interpret their request for help as an admission that they can't fill the job, or worse yet, will pass their concerns on to top management. The fear of not doing it right supersedes asking for help.

- David D. Burns of the University of Pennsylvania turned up a surprising fact: Insurance agents who evaluated their success in terms of their self-worth, job satisfaction, and enjoyment of their work, out-earned agents who evaluated their success entirely in terms of making money, by an average of $15,000 per year.

- Studies show that the chance to grow, learn, and improve skills are among the top five reasons employees give for accepting a new position. Bob Presto, Senior Partner of Korn/Ferry International, the world's largest executive search firm, says high potential employees are more willing then ever before to change companies in order to be part of something important. They want to believe they are making worthy contributions to the group. They want to fulfill their own expectations for growth.

- As Daniel Yankelovich and John Innerwahr wrote in *Work in the 21st Century*, in previous generations people worked to survive. Today, they are increasingly inclined to work as a means of self-expression. Robert Schwartz, founder of Tarrytown Executive Conference Center and the School of Entrepreneurs, estimates that at least 60% of people expect to see their highest ideals and dreams brought to life through their work.

- Craig Finney, associate professor of Recreation and Leisure Studies at California State University, theorized that recreation activities reduced stress on the job and helped people regain control of their lives for a time and consequently have a positive influence on their job. His theory proved correct: *A group spending just 10 minutes playing games after a stressful task out-performed by 300% a group that did not play games.* This finding was also confirmed by a University of Michigan study of employees in 23 occupations.

Trend 3: Incentives for Increased Creativity and Interdependence May or May Not Be Found in Profit-sharing, Ownership, and Incentive Pay Systems

- Edward E. Lawler III, research professor of management and organization, at the University of Southern California, reports productivity increases by 15 percent and 35 percent when incentive pay systems are installed. Yet ordinary compensation and benefit programs simply reimburse employees for their time worked.

- In a survey of *Industry Week* readers, 96 percent said they are in favor of profit-sharing plans, 85 percent said they believe these plans improve employee performance, and 86 percent said they believe the plans improve employee motivation.

- Publicly-held companies that are at least 10 percent employee-owned, out-perform competitors 62–75 percent. Firms owned outright by employees are 150 percent as profitable and have twice the growth rate of other companies.

- A survey of 359 major U.S. companies by Towers, Perrin, Forester, and Crosby (TPF&C), widely respected compensation consultants, disclosed that 84 percent of the respondents used merit, not productivity, as a standard for determining pay increases. They found 41 percent of the companies *do not believe their employees see a link between pay and performance*, and 44 percent do not believe their employees know how their pay is set. They confirmed findings of a 1983 public agenda survey that *77 percent of employees see no direct link between their work and their pay.*

- The United States has more diverse populations of ethnic peoples than any other country in the world. In the U.S., Asians, African Americans, and Hispanics, collectively represent more than $500 billion a year in consumer spending.

Trend 4: The Impact of Globalization Mobilizes Diversity Education and Economic Interdependence

- Hans Koehler, director of Wharton Export Network, says globalization, by definition, requires us to interact with, sell to, or buy from people in other countries who probably speak different languages, and have different cultural and historical backgrounds. He further states that there are two key dimensions to global learning: helping others to open themselves to positive change and developing the ability to value diversity.

- Socrates foresaw globalization when he wrote: "I am not an Athenian or a Greek, but a citizen of the world."

- Gandhi warns us about what we must keep in balance and no longer perpetuate:

Seven Blunders of the World as
Identified by Gandhi

Gandhi's grandson, Arun Gandhi, was sent from his home in South Africa to India to live with his grandfather, Mahatma Gandhi...eighteen months later, before his return to Africa, he was given a piece of paper on which his grandfather had listed his "seven blunders of the world"—mistakes that lead to violence:

- wealth without work
- pleasure without conscience
- knowledge without character
- commerce without morality
- science without humanity
- worship without sacrifice
- politics without principle

Arun adds: • rights without responsibilities and has founded M.K. Gandhi Institute for Non-Violence in Memphis, Tennessee.

- Judith Starkey, author of *Multi-cultural Communication Strategies,* states that global business requires us to think about the importance and impact of building relationships: "Most world societies value long-term relationships over short-term profits...in group-oriented cultures, considerations about the people involved—from management to working class—take priority over the end results."

- The December 1996 issue of *Managing Diversity* cited these global tips for global clients:

    a. respect the local hierarchy

    b. honor relationships before sales

    c. think long-term

- Watt Wacker, futurist consultant, states "In an age of material abundance and uniformity, scarcity becomes more and more valuable. And what's most scarce is difference itself...Do you know what's growing in scarcity? Creativity, being disconnected, patience, face-to-face contact, personalities, heroes...People are eager to buy what has limited availability."

- For the first time in history, thirteen different countries have come together to form the European Commission to formulate an economic alliance. Twelve members of the European Community (Austria, Belgium, Denmark, France, Greece, Italy, Ireland, Luxembourg, the Netherlands, Portugal, Spain, the United Kingdom, and West Germany) have adopted nearly three hundred directives aimed at harmonizing their national defense policies on such issues as banking, trucking, insurance, television broadcasting, taxation, consumer safety, product standards, and the environment.

In 1995, the European Economic Alliance was created to manifest a unified market among these nations—a remarkable feat, and the first of its kind in history. After 2002, the 320 million people who live in European-commissioned countries will constitute the biggest, richest consumer market in the world, with almost as many consumers as the United States and Japan combined.

- Perhaps globalization is a call to developing and recognizing a global spirit that honors all peoples of the Earth. Pat Barrentine's book, *When the Canary Stops Singing*, states this purpose eloquently:

> A global spirit calls forth a sense of integrity in one's life, one's relationships, and one's work; a sense of centeredness and purpose...a sense of compassion—with passion for the suffering of others...a world peace without armed conflict suggests that we as humans can discover new and effective ways to resolve conflict between ourselves and others without use of violence. It's to be said that the history of the world is a record of its wars; however, in a few brief years in the terms of the history of the world, groups that were once enemies and used weapons against each other now consider themselves allies and even friends. We can learn to live without an identified "enemy." As we approach the 21st Century, it seems important to reclaim our history of non-violent responses to, and peaceful resolution of, conflicts.

- How do we mobilize others to reflect awareness of, and sensitivity to, issues of gender, race, and ethnic/cultural diversity? What do we know so far? What resources can we access?

What We Know So Far

Here are some reminders about what we have learned and are learning (by no means comprehensive) with some key resources for us, as we go into the 21st Century:

1. Cultural diversity is a business reality today. The ability to build bridges between people from different countries, with different ethnic backgrounds, is as important as any other business function. Working in a culturally and ethnically diverse organization does not mean eliminating differences in style and approach, but celebrating those differences and tapping into the many strengths diversity brings to an organization.

2. According to Linda Baird, vice president, Human Resources, Bausch & Lomb: "Human-resource people must develop special skills in helping people bridge these cultural barriers—all the old residues of racism and sexism and class and religious differences that people from everywhere bring with them into the work force."

3. Nuala Beck, author of *Shifting Gears: Thriving in a New Economy*, states that the ratio of male to female knowledge workers—engineers, scientists, technicians, professionals, and senior managers—was 3:2 in 1983. Today it is virtually 1:1.

4. Diversity training has the greatest impact when people who work together are trained together.

5. It is different to work through diversity issues if people don't feel comfortable stating unpopular opinions.

6. Diversity-awareness training should be a priority for all employees in order to be globally prepared for business at home and abroad.

7. International studies show that:
   (a) Importance of language skills is an important competitive advantage in today's corporate environment.

(b) "Cultural savvy"—learning to function effectively with people who are different from us—is a necessity.

(c) "Diverse experience" is a real plus in today's résumés—and it's something everyone can acquire, if they don't have it already.

(d) The greatest challenge for championing diversity is backlash (the cause of backlash is fear).

8. The 1994 Hewlett-Packard Corporation Annual Report states that diversity is much more than a program or legal requirement at Hewlett-Packard; it is a business priority. A culture that fosters respect for and appreciation of differences among people clearly helps teamwork, productivity, and morale.

9. Elsie Y. Cross, one of America's foremost diversity consultants, and publisher of the *Diversity Factor*, cites four points for "how to 'do diversity'" in smaller organizations:

- Form a consortium. Small organizations can join up with other groups with similar needs or interests to bring in consultants to help get started. An interorganizational diversity task force might be assembled to design data collection methodologies, create a comparative data base, design strategies, offer training for top-level managers, and evaluate progress.

- Train the trainers. While hiring external personnel to deliver training may be too expensive, the consortium could team up to send people to intensive train-the-trainers programs offered by external organizations.

- Contract for limited co-training work. Trainers in training, or people who have just completed an initial training program, would benefit from opportunities to work with experienced trainers in a sequenced developmental program: observation, participation, guided leadership.

- Join forces to deliver ongoing training. The consortium could develop a strategy that would provide training opportunities for personnel at various levels of the member organizations. Led by a combination of external and internal trainers, these opportunities could be provided at minimal cost to the individual organizations.

10. The research of Ann M. Morrison, founder and president of the New Leaders Institute and author of the 1992 book, *The New Leaders: Guidelines on Leadership Diversity in America,* indicates that a model for leadership development needs to include a balance of three components: challenge, recognition, and support. Relying on challenge alone to develop the leadership potential of nontraditional managers is a dangerous trap. The elements of recognition and support need to be factored in to balance the level of challenge for the leadership development process to be most effective. Perhaps one of the mistakes made in organizations attempting to increase diversity and management is misusing challenge. Challenge is either heaped onto nontraditional managers until they burn out or they are protected from overwhelming challenge, which often contributes to their derailment.

Morrison states most common forms of recognition are: (1) pay, (2) promotion, (3) prerequisites, (4) participation (inclusion in decision making), (5) autonomy, (6) resources, (7) respect and credibility, and (8) faith and trust; and that the most common forms of support are: (1) congeniality; (2) acceptance, acknowledgment, and approval; (3) advocacy; (4) permission to fail or make mistakes and learn from them; (5) information (news about the business and the organization); (6) feedback; (7) flexibility; and (8) stress relief.

Morrison reminds us that businesses and other organizations are in great need of leadership. Discussions about transformation, paradigm shifts, and team performance must also address the reality of cultural differences, sexual and racial prejudices, and other factors that affect how we develop and use leadership talent. These difficult issues are all too often omitted in the dialogue of change agents. We must confront these issues squarely in the new era.

Conclusion

My purpose is to weave and gather the four major trends that are impacting work and relationships in the midst of diversity. Perhaps if we attend to these trends, we can align with researchers, ancient traditions, and the peoples of the Earth, who are pushing for honor, respect, human decency, and global civility. This anthology is a look at possible ways we can create the

"Braided Way," where diversity is respected and, out of our synergetic joining, capacities for communication and people skills are enhanced. The authors in the anthology have addressed the themes of interdependence, new models, and skills that bring attention to and expression of self-esteem, integrity, and enjoyment. Our challenge is to foster creativity that supports cooperative economics for the purpose of creating a global society that values diversity and universal common ground. We have reviewed the trends and research, and we have many resources mobilized in the direction where we are all mutually challenged, recognized, and supported to create a New World Order.

Mikhail Gorbachev was president of the Soviet Union from 1985 to 1991. He is currently chairman of the International Institute for Social, Economic, and Political Studies in Moscow, Russia. He also serves as honorary chairman of the International Green Cross and the Gorbachev Foundation/USA, which hosts the annual State of the World Forum in San Francisco.

His book—*The Search for a New Beginning: Developing a New Civilization*—was published by HarperCollins Publishers in 1995 and was translated by Pavel Palazchenko.

1

On the Edge of a New Frontier

Mikhail Gorbachev

Today, humankind is facing a choice. It is time for every individual, nation, and state to rethink its place and role in world affairs. We need an intellectual breakthrough into a new dimension. And that means that the state of the human spirit assumes paramount importance. The roles of culture, religion, science, and education must grow enormously. The responsibility of the centers of humanity's intellectual, scientific, and religious development is immense and must be given preeminence.

The future of human society will not be defined in terms of capitalism versus socialism. It was that dichotomy that caused the division of the world community into two blocs and brought about so many catastrophic consequences. *We need to find a paradigm that will integrate all the achievements of the human mind and human action, irrespective of which ideology or political movement can be credited with them.* This paradigm can only be based on the common values that humankind has developed over many centuries. The search for a new paradigm should be a search for synthesis, for what is common to and unites people, countries, and nations, rather than what divides them.

The search for such a synthesis can succeed if the following conditions are met:

- First of all, we must return to the well-known human values that are embodied in the ideals of the world religions and also in the socialist ideas that inherited much from those values.
- Further, we need to search for a new paradigm of development that is based on those values and that is capable of leading us all toward a genuinely humanistic or, more precisely, humanistic-ecological culture of living.
- Finally we need to develop methods of social action and policy that will direct society to a path consistent with the interests of both humanity and the rest of nature.

When I speak of a new synthesis, of the need for increasing unity and interdependence, I am not calling for a kind of universal leveling, sameness, or uniformity. I do not accept a civilization that would be like a huge historic steam-roller, flattening out everything. Who would need such a new civilization, and why even call it new? By no means do I want all countries and nations to become alike. *I think that the civilization to which we all belong is one of great multiplicity. And that is a source of its strength,* the basis for the exchange of cultural values, for comparing methods of organization and ways of living.

The philosophy of the twenty-first century must be grounded in a philosophy of diversity. If life as such is the highest value, then even more precious is the singular identity of every nation and every race as a unique creation of nature and human history.

At the same time, we must begin to define certain moral maxims or ethical commandments that constitute values common to all humankind. It is my view that the individual's attitude toward nature must become one of the principal criteria for ensuring the maintenance of morality. Today it is not enough to say, "Thou shalt not kill." Ecological education implies, above all, respect and love for every living being. It is here that ecological culture interfaces with religion.

The beauty and uniqueness of life lies in the unity of diversity. Self-identification—of every individual and of the many different nations, ethnic groups, and nationalities—is the crucial condition for preserving life on Earth. Struggles and conflicts burn out the diversity of life, leaving a social wasteland in their wake. Honoring diversity and honoring the earth creates the basis for genuine unity.

The whole world is at the threshold of dramatic changes. Moreover, this will not be just one more transition from one stage to another, of which there have been so many in history. Many signs indicate that it will be a watershed of historic scope and significance, with a new civilization coming to replace the existing one.

The time has come to choose a new direction of global development, to opt for a new civilization. Today we can only chart its most general outlines. It is a civilization that rules out confrontational approaches. Economic, political, class, interethnic, or ideological wars will have to be abolished. The use of force as a political tool will have to be rejected. Cooperation will gradually supplant competition. It will be a civilization of mutual tolerance, with cultures and nations becoming increasingly open-minded and diversity understood and used as a factor of progress. And, first and foremost, it will be a civilization that assures harmony, and creative coexistence between humanity and the rest of nature.

To build this new civilization, a higher level of responsibility and mutual trust is required among individuals embracing the new order of things. Senior statespeople, current political and spiritual leaders, business executives, scientists, artists, youth, and intellectuals must improve their interaction at both national and international levels.

The statespeople who ended the Cold War established for the first time in modern history the possibility of a truly global peace. In new ways, therefore, our current political leaders are challenged to provide the framework for stability and regulated human interactions; our moral leaders to give expression to the eternal values that have always guided humanity; the business community to assume responsibility for the investment and innovation necessary for prosperity; scientists to take into consideration the ethical and environmental implications of their technological developments; artists to express metaphorically our dreams and tragedies; our youth to demand that the future be better than the past; and intellectuals to offer penetrating insight concerning humanity's progress toward shared goals. *Only the creative interaction of these groups, rather than the supremacy of one group over the others, will allow the answers we all seek to emerge* and guide us as we shape the next phase of human development.

The fact that it is possible to bring such diverse aspects of the human community together, not only in principle but in practice, has been demonstrated recently in the very areas in which trust and cooperation were regarded as unthinkable just a few years before.

There is simply no other way to cope with the current "world disorder," and rampant chaos. The crisis of modern civilization has caused tremendous damage to humankind. It is undermining social ties, family life, moral principles, and values. Many people are acting irresponsibly as though they followed the iniquitous old maxim, "After us, the deluge." The evil of this kind of philosophy and behavior is that it propels humankind toward self-destruction.

In the final analysis the main source of our troubles is not outside, but within us, in our attitudes toward one another, toward society and nature. All the rest derives from that. We therefore must first change ourselves, through self-education and multidisciplinary, worldwide, and cross-generational interaction. And, having changed ourselves, we must come together in all our diversity to build a new world.

My most urgent message is that *it is time for every person and every nation to rethink their role in global development.* Everyone needs to be involved. Everyone has a role to play.

Our political leaders need new overall guidelines. World science alone is not capable of developing them. It is the bringing together of politics, science, religion, and morality that will provide the key to solving the problems that humankind is facing today. And it is the personal involvement of each and every individual that will allow a new civilization to flourish on Earth.

Time and time again I go back to the words of John Kennedy: "We stand today on the edge of a new frontier—a frontier of unknown opportunities and perils, a frontier of unfulfilled hopes and threats." Today, almost thirty years later, we are even more acutely aware that it would be criminal to miss the chance to carry through the historic shifts that have been maturing for so long, and that we vitally need a policy worthy of the scientific and technical achievements of the times and of the new discoveries promised in the century to come.

It is very close, and many of us will live to witness its onset. They say that humanity is always seized by anxiety at the turn of a millennium. Today there is reason for that. The end of the Cold

War, the emancipation of my country and of Eastern Europe, has inspired all of us. But the manifestations of chaos, collapse, and loss of control demand that we bend every effort to seek the paths to an intelligent and necessarily democratic organization of our common abode.

I have no ready-made solutions. I do not believe in imposing models and schemas on society. I believe in the individual, in the potential of intellect and conscience. Like the great American writer William Faulkner, I refuse to accept the end of humankind, however severe our future trials may be.

Riane Eisler is a cultural historian and systems scientist best known for her international bestseller *The Chalice and the Blade*, which has been translated into 17 languages. Eisler is the author of many other books, including the highly acclaimed *Tomorrow's Children: A Blueprint for Partnership Education in the 21st Century*, as well as *Sacred Pleasure; The Partnership Way; Women, Men, and the Global Quality of Life*; and *The Gate*, her memoir of growing up in pre-Castro Cuba after fleeing the Nazi Holocaust.

She has taught at UCLA, Immaculate Heart College, and the California Institute for Integral Studies (CIIS), and is a fellow of the World Academy of Art and Science and the World Business Academy. She is a consultant to schools and businesses on the partnership model she introduced in her work. She has given keynotes for corporations such as DuPont and Volkswagen, as well as to many conferences worldwide. Eisler is president of the Center for Partnership Studies, headquartered in Tucson, Arizona (www.partnershipway.org).

2

Honoring Diversity: Building the Partnership Foundations

Riane Eisler

As we near the twenty-first century, we hear a great deal of talk about honoring diversity in the workplace as a basic ingredient for creativity and flexibility in our rapidly changing world. This is important—and unprecedented. But if it is to be more than just talk, we need to think about the foundations for honoring diversity.

What happens in the workplace does not occur in a vacuum. It takes place in the larger context of all our relationships—in our families and schools, in politics and economics. It also reflects our beliefs, including the images and stories that shape how we view ourselves and others.

What kind of organizational structure and belief system would make valuing diversity possible? What can we do to get from here to there? Are there hidden obstacles in the way?

To answer these questions, we need a clearer understanding of how we are taught to unconsciously equate difference with inferiority or superiority. For instance, we have myths that present half of humanity as inferior to the other or one race as better than another. We also need a clearer understanding of our options for the future, of how honoring or not honoring diversity fits into different futures scenarios. Equally important, we need to take an active part in creating a future when we are no longer conditioned to automatically value one kind of human over another.

The Dominator and Partnership Alternatives

In my research during the past two decades, I have dealt with these issues from a new perspective that makes it possible to see that beneath the great variety of human societies are two underlying configurations or patterns of interactive, mutually reinforcing components. Because there was no existing terminology for these configurations, I coined the terms *partnership* and *dominator* models.

Models are abstractions. But the degree to which a society orients to either a partnership or dominator model has profound implications for all areas of our lives—from the structure of our families, religions, and workplaces to our politics and economics.

For example, societies conventionally viewed as completely different—Khomeini's Iran, Hitler's Germany, Stalin's Soviet Union, and the Masaii of nineteenth-century Africa—have striking similarities. They have three interactive, mutually supporting elements characteristic of societies that orient primarily to the dominator model: a generally hierarchic, top-down, or authoritarian organization; the view that males are superior to females; and a high degree of tension, fear, and institutionalized violence.

By contrast, the partnership model has a different configuration. This configuration also transcends conventional variations in time, place, and level of technological development. Societies orienting more to the partnership model can be found in technologically primitive tribal societies, such as the BaMbuti and Tiruray, and the prehistoric societies I describe in *The Chalice and the Blade* and other books. It is also seen in technologically advanced Western societies, notably the Scandinavian block nations, such as Finland, Sweden, and Norway. In these societies, there is a more democratic and egalitarian social structure. The distinction between male and female is not regarded as the basis for rankings of superiority and inferiority. And because there is no structural need to enforce rigid rankings of domination—be they man over woman, tribe over tribe, or nation over nation—there is less tension, fear, and institutionalized violence.

The Social Construction of Diversity and the Hidden Subtext of Gender

In dominator-oriented societies, children are conditioned to view diversity as either superiority or inferiority; in partnership-oriented societies, they are not. To begin with, in partnership-oriented societies, the universal difference between female and male is not exaggerated by rigid gender stereotypes that divide human traits into impermeable "feminine" and "masculine" categories (thus making it easier to rank one over the other). Children are not socialized to internalize a male-as-master/female-as-subordinate model of our species as a template for in-group versus out-group thinking that can then be generalized to different races, religions, and ethnic groups. Hence, difference is not considered an appropriate reason for excluding members of one gender, race, or other type of group from positions of social governance.

Once we begin to use the partnership and dominator models as analytical tools, we see that how this fundamental difference of gender is treated is a central factor in all aspects of social organization. Since humanity is divided into two different halves, how the roles and relations of these two halves are socially constructed is a basic template for either valuing diversity or automatically equating it with superiority or inferiority.

For example, we see that it is not coincidental that in the classic *The Authoritarian Personality*, social psychologist Else Frenkel-Brunswick demonstrates that individuals who are highly prejudiced against minorities characteristically come from families where there were rigid gender stereotypes—where the father's word was considered law or a "hen-pecking" wife (who was considered an aberration) adopted an authoritarian style. We also see that it is not coincidental that along with the demonstrations in Germany against the hatred and persecution of foreigners during the past two decades has come greater equality for women, and that in earlier more peaceful societies such as Minoan Crete, women along with stereotypically feminine values were not excluded from social governance.

From this larger perspective, it is also possible to understand why societies orienting closely to the dominator model (such as Nazi Germany or Khomeini's Iran) violently persecute those who are different, and why in societies where ethnic wars and massacres occur, there is generally a pronounced male preference. In these societies, female children are not only taught to accept their roles as inferior, but—particularly in places where economic resources are scarce—they are also given less education and health care merely because they were born girls rather than boys.

Moreover, we can begin to understand why in times and places that orient primarily to the dominator model there is an intensified socialization of boys and men to equate their identity or "masculinity" with domination or conquest. For example, this occurred in the West during the years before World War I. As the cultural historian Theodore Roszak writes, it was a period of ever more intense preoccupation with the "horror" of a nation losing "its manhood" (which was equated with militarism and the kind of machismo that ennobles violence and domination).

Moving Beyond Stereotypes

I want to emphasize that none of what we are talking about is a matter of innate male or female characteristics. In other words, we are only talking about gender stereotypes appropriate for a dominator rather than partnership model. Indeed, as we struggle to leave behind entrenched traditions of domination and move toward a more partnership-oriented world, many people today are also trying to leave behind stereotypes that cram both halves of humanity into rigid gender-role straightjackets.

These attempts are central to moving toward the kind of organizational structure—whether in our families or our work-places—where one kind of human is no longer automatically valued more than another.

Thus, in those companies where both women and minority members (including women) are more readily hired and promoted, there is also movement toward a less top-down organization, more teamwork, and a less authoritarian leadership and management style. In these companies there are obviously still leaders and managers, but their roles are defined differently. Specifically, the leader or manager is no longer viewed as someone whose orders may not be disobeyed on pain of severe punishment (the stereotypical definition of the role of the male head of a household). Rather—whether this role is taken by a man or a woman—leaders and managers are defined in more stereotypically "feminine" terms as someone who elicits from others their highest creativity and productivity (a stereotypical mothering role).

These also tend to be companies where stereotypical "women's work" is considered important. They often make provision for child care, parental leave, flex time, and other innovations that enable both women and men to spend more time with their families and take better care of their children.

So if we are serious about creating a workplace—and a world—where diversity can be honored instead of being seen as grounds for prejudice, domination, and violence against others, we need to go more deeply than just what is happening in the workplace. We need to look at the whole social system and the entire fabric of both our conscious and unconscious beliefs. We need to recognize that using diversity as the basis for domination, exploitation, and even violence is not human nature but a cultural pattern. Otherwise, why would some of us reject sexism, racism, and xenophobia along with the scapegoating of immigrants, gays, and the poor? Why would we find, as we do, both modern and ancient societies (for example, the Scandinavian nations and Minoan Crete) that orient more to the partnership rather than dominator model?

The Politics of Diversity

Looking at our contemporary political landscape from a partnership/dominator perspective also makes it possible to understand why those who scapegoat minorities, immigrants, lesbian women, gay men, and the poor for all our economic and social ills oppose affirmative action and make it a top priority to return women to "traditional" roles in a male-headed and controlled family. These are people who have unconsciously, and thus unquestioningly, internalized a model of our species in which one half is ranked over the other. Hence, a core element in their belief system, despite all the rhetoric about individuality and freedom, is the dominator assumption that diversity is the basis for human ranking. This too is why there is so much opposition from these quarters to the education for valuing diversity that has recently been introduced into some of our schools by progressive educators.

In dealing with these attempts to push us backward, it helps if we recognize that prejudices against different "out-groups" are not personal idiosyncrasies but learned attitudes embedded in millennia-old dominator traditions that for the last 300 years more and more people have been struggling to leave behind. It helps to recognize that what we learn in our families, our schools, and our neighborhoods is of profound importance to our lives, both inside and outside the workplace. It helps to pay more attention to dominator messages in the media, where, for example, the devaluation of women is still blatant, as shown by studies of the Annenberg School of Communication documenting that characters on television are two-thirds men and one-third women, and women and minorities are disproportionately portrayed in the role of victims.

Most important, it helps to realize that the underlying struggle for our future is not between conservatives and liberals or science and religion, but between a dominator paradigm, which automatically ranks humanity into those on top and those on the bottom, and a partnership paradigm where valuing difference can be the basis for a less tense and more interesting and creative way of living and working.

So wherever we are, we need to make our voices heard when racist or sexist jokes are told or hate messages are disseminated under the guise of tradition, religion, family values, freedom, individualism, Americanism, or other currently fashionable slogans. If enough of us speak up against prejudice and injustice, we *can* make a difference, both in our workplaces and in the world at large.

The fact that we today hear so much talk about valuing diversity shows that, despite strong resistance and even periodic setbacks, there is movement toward partnership. But if we are to continue our forward movement, we need to redouble our efforts, not only in the workplace, but also in our schools, our churches, our PTAs, our families, our clubs, our legislatures, our courts, our newspapers, and our television and radio shows (particularly our talk shows).

It will take time to change entrenched patterns of belief and behavior. We can accelerate that process by playing a conscious and active part in constructing the foundations for a workplace—and a world—where diversity can truly be honored.

David Goff, PhD, MFCC, co-directs A Foundation for Interdependence, which is dedicated to developing a psychology of interdependence. The Foundation integrates mainstream psychotherapy, transpersonal psychology, and new social learning technologies to create learning communities that catalyze personal empowerment and cultural transformation. The Foundation offers workshops, consultation groups, training seminars, ongoing learning communities, social rituals, and organizational consultation. He also teaches at the Institute of Transpersonal Psychology, where he employs large group processes to promote community and personal development. David's graduate research into the "psychological sense of community" is the first study to describe psychological dimensions of group consciousness. In addition to his writing and ongoing research, he has a psychotherapy practice in Palo Alto, California.

3

The Social Koan:
Through Diversity to
Interdependence

David Goff

At A Foundation for Interdependence, we focus on developing the skills necessary for social interdependence. We see the need for creating community through diversity as a social koan, a paradoxical problem that cannot be resolved without the development of a new mode of consciousness. We focus attention on the dynamic tensions that arise when members of a socially diverse group (or organization) interact. When the members of such a group begin to reflect deeply on these tensions and their responses to them, a process begins that stimulates the emergence of a more complex and interdependent sense of self. In the following discussion we will describe how we use the social koan of diversity to facilitate self-development, cultural awareness, and social interdependence.

A Psychology of Interdependence

The primary mission of our foundation is to develop a psychology of interdependence. Our underlying premise is that humans are embedded in a matrix of relationships that connect us with the larger processes of culture and nature. To the extent that an individual is able to experience these connections directly, they are capable of acting in ways that ensure their own well-being and the health of the natural and social systems they participate in.

Toward that end we have refined the definition of *interdependence*, which has traditionally been defined as "needing and depending on each other." This definition has placed too much emphasis on dependence and is incomplete. An important new level of understanding emerges from examining the prefix "inter," which refers to that which exists "between and among" discrete entities. Beyond depending upon each other, we depend upon what we create between and among us. Instead of stressing dependence (what we can get from our interactions) we emphasize focusing attention on what we contribute to our interactions that enhances the quality of what exists between us.

A psychology of interdependence has two primary areas of emphasis. The first is facilitation of a direct experience of social and ecological interconnectedness. This inoculates the individual against the fragmenting and alienating effects of modern life and is a necessary precondition for the development of an interdependent sense of self. Second, emphasis is placed on skillful interactions. This involves learning how to define and express one's perspective completely. It also involves learning how to open to another's reality. This entails becoming permeable, able to be influenced by another's perspective, while remaining solid and maintaining one's sense of self. How does an individual become both open and solid?

The development of these social skills coincide with the development of a complex sense of self. This cannot be achieved in solitude. We have found that personal complexity evolves through immersion in a social setting that is itself complex and diverse. We have also found that when such a social setting places an emphasis on community, the tensions inherent in community participation necessitates greater clarity about how one defines his or her sense of self.

Learning Community through Diversity

The heart of our work is an experiential educational process called *learning community*. This term gained prominence in the business world through the work of Peter Senge at MIT. He defines learning community as a collaborative learning process that occurs among the primary stakeholders in a "learning organization." In this context such a group functions as a center of self-reflectivity within the organization. Practicing the disciplines of inquiry and reflection, the members of a learning community focus upon increasing the consciousness and coherence of its organizational culture.

We have adapted Senge's approach to address contemporary issues that influence personal and community development. For our purposes a learning community is a group of people who meet together to learn how to function as a community and to create a community in which particular kinds of learning can occur. The task is to create community and then use the collective intelligence of the group to learn new ways of thinking and behaving. As the members struggle to include all their perspectives, they begin to discover what impedes and what furthers their sense of connection. They also reflect upon their interactions and begin to discover more skillful ways of responding to each other.

For our purposes a learning community is a large, ongoing group (sixteen or more members). The group's size provides a critical level of heterogeneity. It also makes the group larger than most people are comfortable with—making it difficult to develop personal relationships with every other member—ensuring that the group remains a place where members interact with unpredictable "others." The ongoing nature of the groups—meeting weekly, biweekly, or monthly over a long span of time—increases the likelihood that the groups cannot rely on a superficial level of compatibility for a sense of connection and presents the challenge of how to create, relinquish, and re-create meaningful experiences together.

The large group also functions as a microcosm of our larger society. Thus we employ it as a small-scale social laboratory where our cultural struggle with differences can be examined. By virtue of the group's need to cooperate for the sake of it's own development and the differences the membership embodies, the social koan is bound to arise. The group will be confronted by the necessity for creating community through its differences.

As the members begin to interact, they soon discover that the way they relate to their differences presents an obstacle to their ability to learn together and collaborate. A learning community does not create a way *around* the tensions that are inherent in the social koan of diversity but rather offers methods so that participants can develop themselves *through* these tensions. By steeping themselves in these tensions rather than rushing to eliminate or resolve them, the members of a learning community engage in a process of psychological and social transformation.

How does this transformation occur? As group members sustain contact with the differing realities of others, they are confronted by the relativity of their own ideas about human nature, relationship, connection, truth, and so on. While the multiplicity of realities is something many people recognize intellectually, actual immersion in a struggle between multiple competing realities presents a very real dilemma. This is a process that arouses a deep sense of existential uncertainty—doubt about the solidity of the ground one's personal and cultural identity is built upon.

How we respond to this doubt determines the quality of interdependence we experience. When we defend ourselves against existential uncertainty by trying to control others or by denying our relationship with them, we generate low synergy (a reduced sense of interrelatedness). This way leads to isolationism, scapegoating, imperialism, and other situations in which "otherness" is devalued and demeaned. On the other hand, we can generate high synergy (increased sense of interrelatedness) in situations when we tolerate the anxiety of uncertainty and develop the strength to occupy our own position while opening ourselves to new realms of complexity, contradiction, and diversity.

Carl Jung described a comparable transformation in his autobiography, *Memories, Dreams and Reflections:* "The more uncertain I have felt about myself the more has grown up in me a feeling of kinship with all things." This special kind of uncertainty arises from an experiential recognition of the limitations and incompleteness of one's construct of reality. This realization provides an incentive for opening the self and allowing it to become more indeterminate and inclusive. Opening to this existential uncertainty, one actually becomes more secure, and in a sense, larger—interconnected with others and experiencing a greater sense of wholeness.

In a learning community the social koan of diversity presents itself as both an obstacle and an opportunity for personal and social development. In the large group, the tensions arising from diversity frustrate and inform, impede and provide transport. They acquaint the participants with direct experience of a special kind of uncertainty as well as a way into a more fundamental ground of interrelatedness.

The Four-Fold Way: Practices for Transformational Learning

The overarching principles we employ with learning communities are found in the Four-Fold Way developed by cultural anthropologist Angeles Arrien. Studying patterns of psycho-spiritual practice across many different cultures, she identified four universal components:

- showing up and choosing to be present
- paying attention
- telling the truth
- surrendering attachment to an outcome

The large group provides a social vehicle for change, and its built-in diversity generates energy. The Four-Fold Way harnesses this energy and utilizes it to propel the members and the group as a whole into new realms of perception and behavior.

A learning community's process transports the group from one view of reality to another, from one form of social orientation to a larger, more encompassing social framework. This kind of learning does not proceed solely through informational training, or through the acquisition of skills, but through transformation—the "emptying out" of an established mindset and immersion in a different experience. As the group explores the tensions associated with community and diversity, it becomes evident that there are no ready, formulaic solutions to these tensions. Participants may well despair about finding a way through these tensions. Remarkably, when they learn how to hang out with their limitations, they come to the place where they become sensitized and discover genuinely new possibilities.

Showing Up and Choosing to Be Present

The first element of the Four-Fold Way describes a minimum requirement for transformation. Nevertheless, it is an exacting practice, involving much more than simply being physically present. Showing up means making yourself known, taking a position by communicating what matters to you about yourself and your experiences in the group and the world. In Arrien's words, showing up requires discipline in the sense of being "a disciple to the self."

Making oneself visible can be anxiety provoking. Many people assume that community means support and confirmation.

This may be true in a community of affinity. In a large and diverse group however, one learns very rapidly that whatever one expresses is likely to be met with a range of responses, including contradiction and conflict. There are no guarantees that others will understand, agree with, value, or validate what is disclosed. Thus, showing up requires striving for self-definition, self-advocacy, and self-expression in the face of disconfirming responses from those who see things differently. To continue to fully show up, members must learn how to validate their own realities without withdrawing from interactions with those who differ. This learning takes time. Members must discover how to manage their anxiety about differing with others, so they can make the contributions to the group that are theirs to make by virtue of their unique perspective.

As the group matures, it becomes clear that something other than a capacity to take a position and assert a viewpoint is necessary for learning to occur. This is where choosing to be present becomes important. Presence means making oneself available to be touched and changed by others. This entails opening oneself to bear witness to others' perspectives, to listen attentively and respectfully, and to be shaped by the variety of contributions others make toward the development of the group. It also means experiencing what is painful, difficult, or incomplete in oneself and in the group.

Choosing to be present asks participants to stay engaged with a process that is beyond their singular control, to share responsibility for what occurs within the group. This challenges the tendency many have to wait for someone else to create an environment that "allows" them to reveal themselves. The goal is not to create special, "hothouse" environments that protect people from the anxieties and risks of taking their unique positions. Instead, a learning community provides a social context where individuals learn to master themselves, so they can tolerate the possibility of conflict or discomfort in order to make their unique contributions to the community's process.

Showing up and choosing to be present is an essential practice in creating community through diversity. It challenges members to bring themselves ever more completely into play and, in the process, to reveal and sustain the experience of diversity in the group. As the members become more proficient at showing up and choosing to be present, they enter the realm of paradoxical tensions that can provide passage to a new way of being together.

Paying Attention

Paying attention is an essential practice without which transformative learning cannot occur. A distinguishing characteristic of a learning community is the quality of consciousness, or attention, that members bring to the task of being together. Increasing awareness sensitizes our perceptions and introduces increasingly subtle levels of reality—and this is what changes the participants.

In the formative stages of a learning community we encourage members to pay particular attention to tension—in oneself and in the group. Since the goal in a learning community is to move toward inclusion and connection, the focus is particularly on the tensions that exist between inclusion and exclusion and between connection and separation. Observing these tensions help group members recognize their own struggles regarding and responding to otherness.

The first tension—between inclusion and exclusion—has to do with who or what is encompassed within the group and who or what is considered unacceptable or outside the boundaries of awareness. The fundamental questions underlying this tension are: "How much differing can be tolerated?" and "How can I (or others) tolerate the uncertainty aroused by differing realities?" Exclusion decreases diversity, therefore diminishing anxiety, but also limiting the scope of the group's potential for learning. On the other hand, inclusion increases anxiety in the group as new information challenges comfortable assumptions and demands the formulation of a more complex picture of reality.

When reality confronts a group (or individual) with more diversity than it can handle, the typical unconscious response is to try to reduce diversity—the encounter with otherness—by excluding something: one's own reality, the other's reality, or the relationship between these realities.

Excluding one's own reality occurs when participants devalue their own viewpoints, hide or silence aspects of themselves, forget what is important to them, are dishonest with themselves or the group, or wait for others to give them permission to make their own contributions (to be themselves). Taking oneself out of the picture minimizes the possibility of differing or conflicting with someone else. It also undermines the feeling of belonging and gives the group an incomplete reality from which to operate. This attempt to minimize diversity tension feeds cultural dynamics such as the segregation and marginalization of those who lack social rank—ethnic minorities, the old and disabled, children, and others.

Excluding another's reality happens when group members try to impose their own perspective on others. This can occur through direct argument and denigration, but it can also happen through persuasion, teaching, healing, analyzing, converting, sympathizing, pitying, generalizing, and asserting rigid rules or "right ways" for participating in community. This attempt to minimize diversity tension feeds and reflects cultural dynamics such as political correctness, fundamentalism, ideological imperialism, and ethnic cleansing.

Excluding the relationship means devaluing the significance of contact and denying the fact that every participant has something unique to contribute. In this case there is an attempt to minimize the impact of encounter by pretending that there is nothing held in common or no way of making a meaningful exchange. This form of exclusion may take the form of abrupt silent withdrawals from membership or a refusal to engage. Slogans such as "you do your thing, I'll do mine," "we'll agree to disagree," "my way, or the highway," all reflect this pattern. On a cultural-political level this pattern is reflected in the self-marginalization of militia groups, cults, and isolationistic national policies.

Each of these forms of exclusion is a way of reducing existential uncertainty by trying to maintain the illusion that there is only one reality, rather than multiple coexisting versions of reality. These responses to differences are toxic to the vitality of a learning community—as well as to social, political, and global communities—because they limit the potential for the evolution of new awareness. Observing these tendencies increases awareness of the underlying roots of many painful cultural dynamics, such as racism, sexism, ethnic conflict, and environmental abuse. As awareness grows, members begin to perceive the parallels between personal choices and group dynamics. They experientially understand the origins of some of the worst symptoms of diversity intolerance. They also discover how their own choices contribute to either reinforcing or altering these dynamics.

Another focal point for attention to the social koan is the dynamic tension which exists between separation and connection. Here, paying attention means focusing upon how we maintain separation and cultivate connection and observing what actually happens within oneself and in the group: How do I

The Civic Quarter Library
www.leedsmet.ac.uk/lis/lss

Borrowed

Customer   Wheatley, Jonathan . (Mr)

                                    Due Date

1 The sociology of w   12/1/2012,23:59
1705436501

2 The future of work   12/1/2012,23:59
700030423X

3 Gender segregation   12/1/2012,23:59
7000403382

4 On work : historic   12/1/2012,23:59
7000314738

5 Working together: 12/1/2012,23:59
1704604969

                      07.12.2011 16:45:24

For renewals telephone (0113) 812 6161
Thank you and see you soon

maintain separation?...When and how do I experience connection?...When does there seem to be an atmosphere of connection in the group?

One of the common notions about connection is that it follows from safety. In a learning community, members discover that actions taken for self-protection usually obstruct contact and generate an atmosphere of distrust within the individual and the group. Members begin to observe how defensive behaviors are often offensive to others. With this awareness comes the realization that our attempts to preserve personal security frequently block us from the sense of connection with others, that maintaining safety—in the sense of invulnerability to others—perpetuates separation rather than connection.

Similarly, as participants pay attention to the actual experience of connection, they are often surprised to find that it arises precisely from situations that might be prejudged as "unsafe." For instance, conflict often feels threatening at first as it highlights the diversity and autonomy of the members. However, as participants use conflict to deepen their positions and presence in the group, they find that they feel more connected and that the group becomes more inclusive. The deepest bonds often arise from the deepest differing.

Another significant awareness regarding separation and connection has to do with the notion that we connect with each other based upon expertise, accomplishment, status, or strengths. In the learning community process, participants are asked to reflect on the ways in which role, rank, and status affect group dynamics and the nature of connection. While accomplishment is valuable, it can also impede the deepest levels of connection based on shared humanity. One of the paradoxes of the social koan is that we must simultaneously bring all of who we are to the interactions, while temporarily suspending our roles and customary identities.

As a group works together over time, the practice of paying attention generates a form of group awareness, or mindfulness. Observing and reflecting on the group's "thinking process," members begin noticing their own judgments and preconceptions. This is important because our assumptions are invisible lenses that filter our perceptions and separate us from direct experience. The *practice of identifying, examining, and suspending assumptions* arouses awareness of the relativity of our perceptions, reminding us that our preconceptions determine what we observe. This practice leads to the fundamental recognition that differing assumptions underlie our relationships and account for much of the confusion and conflict we experience with each other. Paying attention to the effects of our assumptions generates an open and observant form of attention that allows a fresh sense of discernment.

The growing mindfulness of the group reveals the subtle interconnections encompassing individual behavior, interpersonal relations, group processes, and cultural dynamics. The group's attention becomes more focused, creating awareness that is both more penetrating, revealing the nuances of a particular issue, and more encompassing, revealing the larger patterns of which the components are a part. Larger realms of meaning, ordinarily beyond the awareness of a single individual, become accessible. Cultivating this kind of awareness is hard and complicated work. The large group process, with its built-in social diversity, creates both the necessity for developing these attentional capacities and the training ground where they can be fostered.

Telling the Truth

Transformational learning proceeds through the acquisition of a more accurate and comprehensive perception of reality. Telling the truth, like the other elements of the Four-Fold Way, introduces us to unanticipated dimensions of reality.

In a learning community, as in life, the practice of telling the truth starts with discerning one's own position and viewpoint. Truth telling is a way of making one's reality available to become part of the wisdom of the group. As members open up to each other, it becomes clear that truth is far more complicated than any individual's singular perspective.

The emergence of a multifaceted sense of truth is disturbing and leads into the volatile heart of the diversity dilemma. It forces us to confront the realization that our reality is relative—one among many constructed perspectives. The experience of truth's complexity creates a kind of chaos, a cognitive dissonance that disassembles and disorients. Familiar reality is unraveled and we are thrust into an open space where what was once true is now seen as limited. One's reality is both deconstructed and reconstructed by exposure to unfamiliar truths.

Avoiding disturbing truths happens (psychologically and culturally) through two core patterns—denial and indulgence. We practice denial when we insist on the truth that has served us previously and refuse to see what currently is true, or when we deny the realities of others because we fear that we cannot handle the demands new truths will make upon us. We practice indulgence when we dramatize or sensationalize our particular sense of truth, insisting that it is *the* truth rather than *a* truth. In each case we want to avoid experiencing our truth's incompleteness because we fear losing the comfort, security, and equilibrium we find in it. As these patterns occur in the large group, participants find themselves stretched between two desires: on the one hand shielding themselves from the stress of opening to new realities and on the other hand optimizing their learning and connection in the group. Within this tension, transformation occurs, as participants develop greater tolerance for complexity and paradox.

Sharing a multifaceted experience of the moment makes significantly more of the wholeness of that moment accessible. As the diverse facets of the picture become known, these individual perceptions constitute an ever more realistic and integrated image of the whole and make new learning possible. The parts enrich the whole, and the whole in turn gives deeper meaning to the parts. We discover an interconnecting coherence, a more fundamental reality, that exists between singular perspectives but does not become evident until these discrete truths are brought into a dynamic relationship with each other.

Surrendering Attachment to an Outcome

Surrendering attachment to an outcome means emptying out our expectations in favor of opening up to what lies beyond them. This practice is built upon the premise that our attachments and visions of outcome reflect our knowledge and experience of the past; they perpetuate a world that is known and predictable; they protect us from a world that is not. These preconceptions reduce our capacity to respond to the call of the moment, to meet the truths of the present time, to learn. It is for this reason that detachment—the practice of nonattachment or emptiness—is emphasized as a universal spiritual discipline.

Practicing detachment is like voyaging into an unknown sea. Slipping one's moorings loose and setting sail for uncharted waters involves abandoning the safety of the familiar and sacrificing the comforts associated with old ways of knowing. When a learning community sets out together, it is a group of strangers with differing ideas about its destination and method for proceeding. These differing perspectives soon create tensions that manifest as chaos, alienation, and competition for the helm. The temptation for the group (and frequently for the society) is to throw some passengers overboard and elect others as leaders.

What actually threatens the group's journey, however, is the beliefs, prejudices, and preconceptions that have enabled the members of the group to come this far. The primary impediment the group faces is its own anxious desire to avoid relinquishing the safety of the known for the uncertainty of the unknown. The moment of real truth in a learning community comes when members begin to reveal the incompleteness and imperfection of their own knowledge. As they surrender their isolated realities constructed upon partial truths they begin to discover that, despite their pretenses of certitude, they have all along been sailing upon a sea of uncertainty.

This is a terrible liberation. Members find themselves exposed as uncertain, imperfect, and incomplete beings; they experience a vivid sense of openness and existential vulnerability. Difficult as this experience can be, it holds within it a great solace because this very vulnerability is the ground that humanity shares. Through practice, members build the strengths that allow them to be themselves and connect with others in the face of existential uncertainty. Standing upon this ground opens a new vista of self and world, their profound interrelatedness, and a compassionate awareness of the challenges inherent in being human.

Conclusion

As the twenty-first century approaches, humanity stands crowded together at an evolutionary threshold. We are increasingly aware of the *otherness* of those who surround us. At the same time we are beginning to grasp how the political, cultural, and ecological problems that now threaten the survival of our species cannot be adequately addressed without collaboration with them. It seems that we face a dilemma: In order to get along with the business of human existence we must learn how to get along with each other. Can we do it?

At the heart of this question lies a social koan. We face diversity and must discover our underlying commonality. We are presented with threats to our survival and must discover how to take our own positions without the righteous insistence about particular outcomes that inevitably threaten others' survival.

Becoming responsible for a whole larger than ourselves, we must learn how to retain our own integrity without insisting that others forsake their integrity.

Gathering together to address these paradoxical tensions in a face-to-face learning community, we utilize the complications presented by our differences to deliver us to the place where our limited ways of knowing become evident. This is the threshold of an entirely different way of knowing. If we can find the courage to empty ourselves of certainty and open to a world of greater uncertainty, we gain access to a new mode of consciousness and a correspondingly more inclusive and complex sense of self.

When this occurs, group members rediscover the world, and a new sense of the common emerges. Personal well-being and the well-being of the whole are seen to be profoundly interrelated, both depending upon the quality of what we create between us. Access to this new interdependent world is readily available to us. All we need do is turn toward each other and choose to learn what our differences have to teach us about the world we share in common.

Gary W. Janka has worked in the field of management and business for thirty years, the past fourteen as a senior consultant for the Corporate Management Institute in Santa Barbara. The Institute studies organizations and management systems in order to learn and share with clients those methods that lead to effective leadership, improved operating performance, and smoother internal operations. Gary specializes in the design and implementation of Results Oriented Management Systems and the Relational Skills necessary for executives in collaborative, team-based organizations. Clients include companies from a wide range of services and manufacturing industries.

Prior to the Institute, Janka spent sixteen years as a hands-on manager, including such positions as Corporate Controller and Human Resources Director. Janka is currently a doctoral candidate in Confluent Education, which deals with Intrapersonal, Interpersonal, and Intergroup Dynamics.

4

Getting to Know You

Gary W. Janka

Over the many years my colleagues and I have worked with groups doing mediation and team and community building, the one thing I continue to be impressed by is how tenaciously self-referential we humans are. By self-referential I mean the tendency we have to use ourselves as the reference point for judging what is right, proper, and preferred. By using ourselves as the reference point, we expect others to see the world the way we see it, to make decisions the way we make decisions, and to do things the way we would do them. And, of course, they don't. Others do it their way. Therein lies the rub. So the question we are constantly faced with as professionals is how do we help individuals with different worldviews, different values, and different decision-making processes develop enough common ground and mutual acceptance to collaboratively complete a task.

In 1992, when serious riots broke out in Los Angeles following the acquittal of the officers involved in the beating and arrest of Rodney King, my colleagues and I were reminded of how terrible the consequences of our self-referential tendencies can be. We thought it might be useful to develop a process that could bring together people of different cultures and give them a gentle, safe, and enjoyable way to explore their perceptions of each other and, perhaps, begin to develop a common agenda. It was our hope that the process would be used to build bridges in racially or ethnically diverse neighborhoods, to become a sort of "block-building" or community-building program. (Over time we have found the process has more far-ranging applications and can be used in any situation where the people involved have different points of view and a need for common understanding, even with a group of "old white men.") Given our professional inclination toward implementation and practical application, we looked into our experience to see what we had found effective.

We understood well that the pathway to change begins with an *awareness of self*, a clear picture of our ways of looking at the world, our ways of making decisions, our value priorities. If I am not clear about the lens through which I view the world and my own value priorities, I will not be able to relate to those of another or those of an organization. The second step on the path is to develop an *awareness of others*, to begin to see and understand the other person's lens and value priorities. Following awareness comes the *acceptance* of the fact that your lens is different from my lens and your value priorities are different from mine. Once the acceptance is there, we can take the next step, which is the *appreciation of differences*. Not only can I accept that you and I see the world differently, but I can begin to appreciate that you bring something to the party that I do not. None of us has it all, and we can begin to see that there is much more strength in our togetherness than in our separateness. Finally, if the other stages are in place, we can begin to *constructively use our differences* in a very conscious manner.

Carl Jung, the Swiss psychiatrist, is said to have once remarked that "being truly understood by another human being is one of life's rarest experiences." So, along with following the natural change process of *awareness—acceptance—appreciation*, we also knew that it was essential to focus on the skills and the discipline necessary to achieve mutual understanding. Toward this end, we built in some training on what we refer to as the Professional Dialogue Process or PDP. (A summary of this process is in Appendix B.) The important point here is to ensure that each participant is both able and required to clearly articulate the other's point of view before presenting his or her own. This helps us get beyond our natural tendency to explain, refute, deny, argue, or persuade without truly understanding the other person.

Finally, in designing our process, we knew from experience that talking about something is spectacularly ineffective in causing change. It may be useful in creating a level of cognitive awareness and even causing some insight to occur, but to bring about fundamental change at the intrapersonal level, it is essential to engage people both intellectually and affectively. That is, it's essential to get them "neck deep" in both their *thoughts* and *feelings* about the issues, their perceptions, and their value priorities. Our reactions to others and to a given situation almost never lie in others or the situation. The roots of our reactions (behaviors) lie in the thoughts and feelings we have *about* others and the situation.

What follows is a description of the process we developed based on these principles and understandings. (An outline version is in Appendix A.) It can be used with just about any group or collection of individuals where the desired outcomes are increased understanding, acceptance, and appreciation of others. It is helpful to have a balance between subgroups (racial, ethnic, gender, age, etc.), and it is helpful to have an even number (twelve to sixteen) of participants. It is designed to be done in three separate events, each three to four hours long, and it can also be done quite well in a weekend retreat. We prefer to carry out the process in a "home-like," relaxed atmosphere free from outside distraction. Someone's living room or a hotel suite would work well. It's also helpful to have access to a kitchen as it's powerful to build in the sharing of food.

Session One

I usually start by welcoming the participants and talking a little about the purpose of the process, how and why it was developed, and what the hoped-for outcomes are, taking time to validate the outcomes with participants to see if that's why *they* are present. If there is a disconnect or some strong feelings about being there (anxiety, resentment, and so on), we can take some time for the group members to decide how they want to deal with them. It's also useful to take some time to review the process agenda and talk about any logistical matters. If there is to be a set of "ground rules" in place, this is a good time to review and, if necessary, modify them. Use your own judgment and knowledge of the group to determine what ground rules would be appropriate. One I have found particularly useful in this setting is: "You don't have to do anything you don't want to do except stay in the room and follow the other ground rules." This gives the participants a great deal of freedom and security.

As a way of introductions, we suggest the "how did you get your name?" process. Almost everyone has a story to tell about how he or she was named. For example, when I was born (1943), one of the hot actors was Gary Cooper of *High Noon* fame. Since my mother was, shall we say, impressed with him, I was named Gary. Having people talk about how they got their names is a gentle, fun way of helping them get to know each other in a very personal way.

The next thing I usually do is to have people choose partners, preferably someone they do not know well or work directly with, and sit facing each other. I ask them to sit as close to each other as they feel comfortable and then just a little closer. It's nice if their knees can touch each other's chairs. I ask them to sit with their feet flat on the floor and their hands palm-down on their thighs. I also ask them to try to maintain eye contact without staring, to take time to really see the other person, to notice the highlights in their hair, the texture of the fabric they are wearing, and so on. While they are sitting like this, their task is to just notice what they think and feel, both physically and emotionally. Typically almost everyone nervously giggles, smiles, laughs, and fidgets. It is very hard for most people to just sit and not feel compelled to talk or do something with this person in front of them.

After a couple of minutes, ask them to disengage and share with the group what it was like for them to just be with their partner. Some will talk about their discomfort, others about their pleasure. The point of this process is to simply have people experience what it is like to be in close proximity with another (hopefully quite different) person without a task to accomplish. It is helpful for them to begin to realize that what they experienced is always present when we have to work with another person. We adopt polite behaviors, keep our distance, and focus on the task as a way of minimizing or masking the feelings or thoughts we just experienced. As our awareness grows of what is present in our being together and we can begin to accept as well as appreciate it, we can also begin to turn loose of it. This frees us up to fully focus on the other person and the task at hand.

After debriefing on the "being with" process, I take a few minutes to explain and demonstrate the Professional Dialogue Process. As a first practice session, I usually do an abbreviated version. I ask people to pair off again (with the same partner) and face each other as before. One person is the Sender and the other the Receiver. The Sender's job is to finish the following sentences:

- "Right now I'm (physically) feeling..."
- "Right now I'm thinking..."
- "Right now I'm (emotionally) feeling..."

The Receiver's job is to respond to each statement by "mirroring" or reflecting back what the message the Sender sent. For example,

- "I hear you saying that..."
- "I understand that you..."
- "Right now you're..."

Give the Senders one or two minutes on each statement, announcing the time to shift, then tell participants to reverse roles. The Senders become the Receivers and repeat the process.

After each person has had the chance to both send and receive, ask them to disengage and again share with the group what it was like for them, what they experienced.

If you have arranged for a meal, this is a good time to eat. The experiences people have had will be sufficient to loosen them up and give them many conversation starters to encourage talk during the meal.

After the meal, announce "game time" and ask everyone to divide themselves up into mixed groups of four to six people each. Each group should have its own copy of a game called Life Stories (see Appendix C) and a separate table on which to play. The cards the players draw ask them to tell something about themselves, and we have found it a wonderful way to help people begin to know each other in very human ways and at a much deeper level than they normally would in a first encounter. The game rules allow players to put a card back and choose another if the question it asks is not one they feel comfortable answering. You will hear some very delightful stories, sometimes funny and sometimes sad. Playing the game creates a safe space for people to share of themselves, and I have trouble keeping my copies of it. The participants always buy them from me at the end of the session!

After all the groups have completed the games, reassemble participants in a large group and take them through a simple debriefing. How was it for them? What was the funniest story in each group? What was the biggest surprise? What did you learn about yourself? What was your comfort level as you told your stories? Many times even more sharing is done as people relate their experiences.

To begin wrapping up this first session, I usually express my appreciation for the work they have done together and ask them to choose a partner (preferably a different one from before) and sit facing each other. A simple appreciation process works well here and is another opportunity for people to practice the PDP. The Sender's job is to express appreciation of the other person. For example,

- "I appreciate your willingness to tell the story about the time your father caught you smoking behind the garage."
- "I appreciate the beautiful blue tie you are wearing."

The Receiver's job is to simply mirror or reflect the appreciation:

- "I hear you saying that you appreciate my telling the story about..."
- "I understand that you appreciate my blue tie."

The appreciation can be about anything the Sender sees or feels. Give everyone enough time before switching roles to cause people to become creative and get beyond the obvious stuff.

At this point the first session is finished. Be sure to allow people time to hang around and talk some more as they are often inclined to do so. Relationships are starting to form. If there is to be a meal in Session Two, consider making it "potluck" and ask participants to bring a dish that represents them or their group as a way of emphasizing diversity.

Session Two

I usually begin the second session with a simple "check-in" or warmup of some kind. Asking people to share a significant event that happened since last time, an insight they had, or just what is going on with them right now is enough to break the ice and start the session going. I am sometimes amazed at the depth of sharing at this point even though the group has only had one session together. It's also useful to have people restate their names as memories can generally use the refresher.

Before moving into the "main event" of the session, I have also found it helpful to provide the participants with some additional practice with the PDP and to do it in a way that encourages additional sharing of personal history. I ask them, individually, to recall an event in their life (involving someone who is not in the room) around which they still have some leftover feelings. It may have been a situation they are still angry, sad, or resentful about. Whatever it is, when it is their time to be the Sender, they are to consider the Receiver a surrogate for the person with whom they have the "leftover" issue. They will need to take a minute to brief the other on the general circumstances surrounding the incident. As the Sender, their job is to communicate to the Receiver what they felt at the time of the real incident and what they are feeling now. The Receiver's job is to *mirror— validate—empathize.*

Give them three to five minutes, then have them reverse roles. Allow more time if you feel it is needed. This approach causes the participants to communicate with each other at the level of feelings rather than ideas. As feelings are more universal and "in-common" than the ideas we have about each other, a tremendous amount of empathy and trust can begin to build in the group. As before, it helps if the two people in the dialogue are from different subgroups. I also encourage people to pick someone they have not yet worked with so the bonds can begin to broaden within the group.

At this point, ask the participants to break up into their "natural" subgroups (men-women, black-white, straight-gay, and so forth) and to prepare for the "See You/See Me" process. If a person identifies with more than one group, he or she should choose a group that feels comfortable. To prepare, ask each subgroup to move into its own work space (tables are helpful, as is some distance between groups) and to create three lists of perceptions on separate sheets of easel paper. The three sheets should be headed:

- How We See *Ourselves*
- How We Think *You* (the other subgroups) See *Us* (our subgroup)
- How *We* See *You* (the other subgroups)

If there are more than two subgroups present, ask them to prepare additional sheets for each subgroup relative to bullets two and three. The point here is to have them identify and articulate all the assumptions, beliefs, and stereotypes they have about people in the different subgroups. I laughingly tell them they do not have to be "nice," and they should be honest. There is often much anxiety around this process, particularly if there have been hard feelings between the subgroups in the past. Keep reassuring them that this is a safe place to share their perceptions and that our purpose here is to drive for understanding, not to refute, deny, criticize, or even change minds. As facilitator, move around to the various subgroups and keep it light.

After each subgroup has had an adequate time to develop its lists, ask people to stay together in their subgroup and to rejoin the other subgroups for some dialogue about what they have prepared. As you can probably anticipate, if there are more than three subgroups, the ensuing dialogue can be complex and lengthy, so take that into account when planning the events.

Once the subgroups have come back together, ask each to present its How We See *Ourselves* sheet to the others, encouraging full explanation by the presenter(s). One additional ground rule I impose during this process is that the people being presented to can only ask questions of clarification and understanding. They are not allowed to refute, criticize, or explain. Once each subgroup has had an opportunity to present how they see themselves and there is common clarity, ask people, as a large group, to identify what they see in themselves that they *have in common.* You will typically find they share more attributes than not. If you observe any striking or important differences, you may want to bring them out and open them up for some exploration and dialogue.

Now that each subgroup has had a chance to report how they see themselves, ask one subgroup to take the next step by presenting to the others How We Think *You* See *Us.* As before, the Receivers can only ask questions of elaboration, clarification, and understanding. If there are several subgroups, have the Senders complete all of their lists. At this point, the Receiving subgroups become the Senders and present to the subgroup that just sat down their How *We* See *You* sheets. It's best to have them go one at a time so an orderly dialogue will be achieved. Before having the second subgroup present their How We Think *You* See *Us* sheets, it's good to have a short period of open discussion about what participants have just shared with each other. There may be additional questions or perceptions that are not yet fully understood. As long as the discussion is flowing well and well intended, I tend to let it flow. If it begins to become tense or emotional, I may invoke strict PDP structure to ensure the search for mutual understanding can continue in a safe and "contained" way.

If there is to be a meal break, you will have to work it in at a logical break point. If you do the diversity potluck, ask participants to talk about their dish and tell what it represents in terms of the them or or their group.

After each of the subgroups has sent and received, it is good to spend a few minutes processing what was presented and discussed. You might ask questions such as:

- What did you *hear*?
- Were there any *surprises* in the way others see you?
- What did you *feel* as others were telling you about how they see you?
- How did you *interpret* what you heard? (i.e., What judgments, evaluations, imputed motives did you add to what was said?)
- Can you identify where these perceptions came from, how you got them?

For many people this will be the first time they have had an open sharing of perceptions with someone of another subgroup, and the effect can be rather profound. Often the group is reluctant to break up and the conversations can go on for hours. This is the material from which trust is built. If I do not really know what you think of me, it's hard for me to trust you.

For a closing, I like to use a variant of the Appreciations Process we used in the first session. This time, instead of expressing appreciation of the other, the Senders should complete the statement:

- "What I want to be appreciated for is..." or "I want you to appreciate me for..."

The Receiver's job is to mirror the request by appropriately completing the statement:

- "I appreciate you for..."

One added touch to consider: Many people have never made physical contact with a member of a particular subgroup. For example, many white people have never touched a black person or a straight male may never have touched a gay male. Being very mindful of possible gender issues, consider having the people do this closing process standing up with one or both hands on each other's shoulders. Expect a few tears.

Session Three

For some of the participants, the third session may seem a little anticlimactic after the intense sharing that typically occurs in Session Two. And, it is quite necessary to consolidate the awareness into learning and translate the learning into concrete change.

As before, a simple opening process or icebreaker that causes people to work together in mixed groups will do. I particularly like Band Together, developed by Sue Forbess-Greene (see Appendix C) because it draws on the right side of the brain and is a great "equalizer." The process involves giving each group a set of previously prepared cards that bear the name of a musical instrument. Each group is to distribute the cards by whatever means they choose and each individual is to pretend to play the given instrument by mimicking its sound. Each group should then retire to a private space to choose a song, and a "conductor" and then rehearse. Give them 10 to 15 minutes. Each group should then rejoin the others and play for them the song they rehearsed. This one is always good for a few laughs and exposes our humanness. The applause is typically genuine and heartfelt.

Following the warmup, we do a more serious activity, typically a game or simulation that is relevant for the group. The purpose of this is to continue their exploration of stereotypes as well as their awareness of the underlying perceptions. (There are a large number of games and simulations available on the market and I have listed my favorites in Appendix C.) Feel free to use whatever you have found successful in the past and to choose one you feel is appropriate. I prefer to look for one people can play or work on in mixed groups rather than separate subgroups at this stage of their development.

The game or simulation should be followed by a debriefing period to give the participants an opportunity to sort out their feelings and digest any new awareness or insight. Such process questions as:

- "What did you hear?"
- "How did you feel?"
- "How does this remind you of everyday life?"

are usually quite adequate to begin a meaningful discussion. Allow sufficient time for everyone to have a chance to participate.

If you are going to take a meal break, this is a good place to do it. As I use the second meal to emphasize diversity, it's good to use this meal to emphasize commonality. One way to do so is to give assignments at the second session for dishes to be prepared by two or three people working together. Another way is to make it a "theme meal" that is somehow relevant to the group. For example, with a group of new immigrants, you might want an "All American Meal." Many times the group will want to develop its own theme.

Next, we want to accomplish two things: to help people focus on what unites them (their common interests) and second to identify something they can work on together to change or improve their situation.

Begin by asking the group to reassemble into mixed triads and ask them to discuss and record (on easel paper) their collective responses to the following questions:

- "What have you learned from our work together?"
- "What has changed for you since we began this process?"
- "What would you like to accomplish as a result of what you have learned?" Or, "How will you use what you've learned in daily life tomorrow and the day after?"

Give them ten minutes to develop their responses and then have the triads share their responses with the others. Ask someone to serve as recorder. Focusing on the "What would you like to accomplish?" list, work with the group to see if they are able and/or ready to identify some concrete and common undertaking.

A community group may decide to have monthly block potlucks to build and nurture relationships. Another may choose to work on a Neighborhood Watch Program or to set up a safe place for their children to go after school and do their homework. An intact work group may identify ways of altering their meeting processes to accommodate individual differences. A nonintact work group may want to jointly develop a proposal for a new employee orientation program to ease the assimilation of minority subgroup members, and so forth. Not every group will identify something they want to work on in common, so the emphasis may have to be on individual change and implementation. The important thing is to help the participants translate the learning and insight into behavior.

After what is often an intense and emotional experience for the participants, it is good to have an expressive closing. There is one I like that I am told comes from the Sufi tradition. It involves having participants form two concentric circles, the inner circle facing outward and the outer circle facing inward. There should be an equal number of people in each circle so each can face another. At the initiation of the facilitator, the group begins to sing a simple song together, incorporating the indicated body movements. The words and movements are as follows, you can make up your own tune:

> *To you I give.* (Hands held upright, palms facing the person opposite.)
>
> *From you I receive.* (Hands held out, palms facing up.)
>
> *Together we share.* (Arms folded across chest, hands on own shoulders.)
>
> *And we all give thanks.* (Hands in front, palms and fingers together, tips of fingers level with tip of nose.)

At the conclusion of the verse, the participants give each other a small bow with their hands held in front of them and the outer circle rotates one person to the left. The song is repeated as many times as there are pairs of people.

Some Final Thoughts

This simple yet effective process helps people build bridges between different cultures and divergent points of view. In closing, I think it is important to share some additional thoughts about its design.

First, there is a conscious recognition that some of the things the process asks or encourages people to do may be inherently uncomfortable or even contrary to the norms of the participant's culture. For example, in some cultures it may be considered impolite to maintain eye contact or for a man to sit close to a woman who is not his wife. It may be considered culturally improper to talk openly about what one is feeling or to show feelings in a group. It is important to appreciate that a primary purpose and intent of the process is to make the implicit explicit. That is, to facilitate the movement of normally unconscious perceptions, beliefs, and taught behaviors into the realm of conscious observation and discussion. We *want* these differences to come to the surface so that they may be understood, accepted, and appreciated. So in this regard, the process is intended to be mildly provocative; it's okay for people to feel uncomfortable. At the same time, it is essential that the facilitator be observant and use any discomfort or reluctance as a productive opportunity for developing awareness.

Second, this process was designed with the assumption that the participants are interested in the opportunity to do some bridge building and want to do so. It also expects that there may have been a mild level of past conflict or misunderstanding between individual participants or subgroups. If, however, there is a known history of overt conflict and hostility, you may want to consider modifying the process or doing some preparatory work with the participants in another setting to define issues and build a more structured agenda. Perhaps some one-on-one work with the Professional Dialogue Process would be appropriate or a more traditional mediation approach used instead. Please make the effort ahead of time to take a good reading on the participants and the situation they have been living with.

And finally, I believe the process is the easy part. The hard part is creating the opportunities for people of different races, ethnicities, economic groups, and religions to come together for this kind of exploration and community building. As I look at the way society functions, particularly with the growth of isolating technologies such as television, videos, and computers, we tend not to mix much with people outside our group beyond those we may work with. As change agents, we have a responsibility to actively look for opportunities to cause people to come together, and it should not take a destructive riot to do it. The worksite is an obvious avenue for building bridges as are schools and coalitions of religious organizations. Perhaps you will think of others. Please take this process and use it. The world could use it.

Appendix A

"Getting to Know You"
A Process Overview

Session One
- Welcome, logistics, review of process
- "How did you get your name?" process
- Introduction to the Professional Dialogue Process
  —Practice Session
- Play Life Stories game
- Debrief
- Close with "Appreciations" process

Session Two
- Ice breaker or warmup process
- Practice with Professional Dialogue Process using past event
- Preparation for "See You/See Me" process
- Presentation of perceptions
- Debrief and process responses
- Close with second "Appreciations" process

Session Three
- Ice breaker or warmup
- Play diversity game or conduct simulation exercise
- Debrief and process what flows out of the game or simulation
- Begin wrap-up: Identify learning and translate into concrete action.

** Build in meals and breaks where appropriate.

Appendix B

Professional Dialogue Process

Sender: The one who wants to send a message must take the initiative and say:

"May I have a professional dialogue with you?"

There are two reasons to have one:

1. You are upset and want to discuss it.
2. You have a topic to discuss and want to be sure you are heard and understood.

Receiver: The Receiver should grant a dialogue now if possible. If not now, set a definite time so the Sender knows he/she will be heard. The Receiver does three things:

First: Mirror what the Sender says:

"What I heard you say is... "

When there is a natural pause, ask:

"Did I get it right?" and "Is there anything more you want to say about that?"

If the receiver is feeling overload, he/she may signal for a pause.

When the Sender has finished sending, the Receiver moves on to:

Second: Validate the person by summarizing what has been said and follow with a statement like:

"I've heard what you said and you make sense to me." "You make sense to me" is the important part.

Third: Empathize by letting the person know you understand what he/she is *feeling* about the situation. Something like:

"I imagine you might be feeling..." or "I imagine you might have felt..."

Then take a guess at what the person is or was feeling (angry, upset, confused, sad, frightened) and check it out:

"Is that what you are/were feeling?"

Mirror what is said and stay in the process until the Sender is satisfied he/she has been heard, understood, validated, and empathized with.

At this point the Receiver may wish to ask:
"What were you expecting from me at that time?" or "What do you want from me now?"

Be specific about the behavior you want (i.e., make a behavioral change request).

Then mirror, validate, and empathize as you did before.

When the Sender feels complete, the Receiver may say: "I want to respond now."

The two people now switch roles. The receiver becomes the sender and the process repeats itself.

—Adapted from works by Harville Hendrix, PhD
and Marshall Rosenberg, PhD

Appendix C

Favorite Resources

There is a wide variety of materials available to practitioners, and I encourage you to build in and use those you have experience with and have found effective. These simply happen to be the ones I've found work well for the purposes of the "Getting to Know You" process.

1. The Band Together icebreaker comes from a book called *The Encyclopedia of Icebreakers* by Sue Forbess-Greene. It is published by University Associates, 8517 Production Avenue, San Diego, CA 92121.

2. I sometimes prefer to use task-oriented simulations instead of games, particularly those having to do with survival situations because they emphasize our interdependence. Living in California, a natural for me is Earthquake from Aviat in Ann Arbor, MI. Call (800) 421-5323 and they'll be happy to send you a catalog. They have lots of other good stuff too!

3. For games, I suggest one of the following:
    - Same Difference from Diversity Simulation Games by Sivasailam Thiagarajan, PhD.
    - First Thoughts (#18) from 50 Activities for Diversity Training by Jonamay Lambert and Selma Myers.
    - When I Felt Different (#4) from 50 Activities for Managing Cultural Diversity by Terri Dickerson-Jones.
    - If I Could Go Back (#5) from 50 Activities for Managing Cultural Diversity by Terri Dickerson-Jones.

    All four of these games are available from HRD Press, 22 Amherst Road, Amherst, MA 01002. HRD offers a wealth of materials relative to diversity education. If you're not familiar with their materials, I suggest you call for their catalog; phone (800) 822-2801.

4. The Life Stories game is manufactured by Talicor, Inc., in Pomona, CA 91767; phone (800) 433-GAME.

Dianne Crampton is the founder of TIGERS Success Series and the TIGERS core value-based group development model. TIGERS addresses behaviors that support six essential values inherent in all vibrant, caring, quality-focused, ethical and successful teams. The six values are trust, interdependence, genuineness, empathy, risk, and success.

TIGERS has been recognized by the United Nations Secretariat for creating a human resource model that promotes intergenerational cooperation and caring. Crampton's work with Native Americans was featured at a UN-sponsored conference in Minneapolis, Minnesota.

In 1995, Merrill Lynch Corporation nominated Crampton for *Inc.* magazine's Entrepreneur of the Year.

Bringing more than 18 years of project development, training, facilitation, and public speaking to her model, Crampton lives with her husband Bill in Bend, Oregon. Her website is www.corevalues.com.

5

Interdependence: A Matter of Practical Diversity

Dianne Crampton

The training room quieted. Participants clustered around the conference table, glanced at one another, then back to me. Ethically, how would I respond?

I had been commissioned to discuss personality diversity and the role practical differences play in conflict resolution with a public education union team. Due to public education's emphasis on administrative decentralization and a shift of decision-making power to individual school building staffs, the union team's role was expanding. As school districts moved to adopt site-based councils, union roles broadened to embrace both teacher advocacy and team-process education.

The role expansion was in direct response to schools forming teams to strategically plan and solve building problems. The site councils required timely information on how to interact in ways that balanced work requirements with interpersonal awareness and good team skills. Principals and teachers who once enjoyed a hierarchical decision-making process, independent classroom management roles, and faculty information meetings were now expected to relate with one another in different and more collaborative ways.

A union team member's provocative question hung in the air. "Why do I have to give up who I am in order to make our meetings work?" I contemplated my answer.

This is the type of ethical question stretching the values of today's workers. Here it involved a leap from an established organizational paradigm to a new one—from centralized control, competition, and independence to shared control, collaboration, and interdependence. And, as an organizational culture makes such leaps, rigid individualists become potentially less effective than collaborative team members whose competence expands as they explore ways to become more effective with greater numbers of people and circumstances. While the question of modifying behavior to increase a group's effectiveness may imply personal loss, increasing one's interpersonal effectiveness implies gain. The gain is felt not only in group success but also in personal and group power. The question rotated around a central point: Was I requesting that people change or asking them to be all they could be?

The TIGERS "I"

In 1987, I asked a life-transforming question. What is necessary to build an ethical, quality-focused, productive and successful group of people? Searching for the answer led me into an intense review of three disciplines—psychology, education, and business. From this study six universal principles of healthy group dynamics emerged—Trust, Interdependence, Genuineness, Empathy, Risk, and Success in implementing a group's goals and procedure, from which I coined the acronym TIGERS® and from which TIGERS Success series, a core values-based team consulting business, emerged.

In a 1991 study involving the six principles, I learned that interdependence and success are highly correlated with the other TIGERS values. If either interdependence or success is reinforced, the other TIGERS values will be as well. Interdependence balances the work and relationship equation and creates a synergy that bonds a team together with greater power and effectiveness.

Interdependence relies on sharing, openness, acceptance, respect, support, and wholeness. It means that two or more people appreciate and rely on one another's strengths and are mutually responsible for personal limitations. Accordingly, people must be willing to be self-reflective and accountable for their relationship and work actions. Because interdependence requires self-awareness and appreciation for others, it demands high levels of self-security and self-esteem from team members. This builds reverence and respect that elevates human interactions.

Interdependence is based on the idea that if we win, I win. Interdependence is, therefore, essential for:

- effective interpersonal communication
- problem solving and critical thinking
- teamwork
- collaboration

It demands respect for other people's rights, beliefs, likes, dislikes, and vulnerabilities. Interdependence asks us to begin honoring people as a whole.

Geese in flight present a natural example of interdependence. Reverend Todd Fast, an Episcopal priest from Seattle, Washington, offered the following discussion on geese at a Seattle Downtown Rotary presentation:

> Do We Have as Much Sense as a Goose?
>
> This spring when you see geese heading back north for the summer flying along in a "V" formation, you might be interested in knowing what scientists have discovered about why they fly that way. It has been learned that as each bird flaps its wings, it creates an uplift for the bird immediately following. By flying in a "V" formation, the whole flock adds at least 71 percent greater flying range than if each bird flew on its own.
>
> *BASIC TRUTH #1: People who share a common direction and sense of community can get where they are going quicker and easier because they are traveling on the trust of another."*
>
> Whenever a goose falls out of formation, it suddenly feels the drag and resistance of trying to go it alone and quickly gets back into formation to take advantage of the lifting power of the one immediately in front.

BASIC TRUTH #2: If we have as much sense as a goose, we will stay in formation with those who are headed the same direction we are going.

When the lead goose gets tired, he rotates to the back and another goose flies point.

BASIC TRUTH #3: It pays to take turns doing hard jobs - with people or with geese flying north.

The geese honk from behind to encourage those up front to keep up their speed.

BASIC TRUTH #4: We need to be careful what we say when we honk from behind.

Finally, when a goose gets sick, or is wounded by gunshot and falls out, two geese fall out of formation and follow him down to help and protect him. They stay with him until he is able to fly or until he is dead, and then they launch out on their own or with another formation to catch up with their group.

BASIC TRUTH #5: If we have the sense of a goose, we will stand by each other like that.

Acceptance, support, sharing, openness and respect are important values in understanding the team interdependence equation: $1 + 1 > 2$. It is why geese fly in a "V" formation. The formation increases their efficiency by 71 percent. It also enables the geese to set a challenging pace.

The willingness to explore one's strengths and limitations through self-reflection and group accountability also allows team members to increase their personal and group success. For example, if team members become aware that their impatience causes them to interrupt team discussions, they can write their thoughts down to interject after the speaker has finished. This builds respect between people and aids the process. Self-correcting team members also benefit by developing more effective communication and listening skills.

In another example of self-awareness, people may become aware of their failure to get to the point in their discussions. Focusing their thoughts and comments before talking fosters respect between people and builds team efficiency. It also helps to keep discussions on track and reduces perceptions of interrelational manipulation. Self-correcting team members also benefit by developing stronger communication and group assertiveness skills.

Self-awareness and self-correction help to bridge the reality that people are vastly different. We think differently. We look different from one another. We have different cultural and personal experiences. We look at the world and react to it differently.

For example, some people are extroverted and gain considerable energy from being around people. They form opinions spontaneously and in interaction with others. Others are more introverted. They thrive alone or in less interactive situations. They also carefully think things through before forming opinions and take time in forming their thoughts.

On another level, some people are very businesslike and power oriented. They are disciplined and require documented evidence stressing results. Others are more open and friendly. They are interested in knowing who people are, what they think, and who they know. They appreciate recognition and approval. Some are very honest and sincere. They require evidence that others are trustworthy and nonthreatening. They appreciate safety and require demonstrations of personal attention and interest. Many people are task oriented. They demand evidence of competency in solving problems and analyzing situations. They also require evidence that people have done their homework and are accurate in their findings. Clearly, people have different knowledge bases and have developed different skills to cope with the world. When we work with the strengths of these differences, the dynamics are fantastic.

Through its diversity, a high-functioning interdependent team becomes more well-rounded and potentially wiser than one whose members are coerced into conformity by competitive means. By respecting individual integrity, educating one another about our different cultural experiences, and respecting individual strengths and leadership styles, a high-functioning team is a formidable force to reckon with.

One organization that has excelled at defining and complementing people's strengths and opportunities for growth is

Humanix Temporary Services. Humanix and owner Julie Prafke were recognized in 1994 by *Inc.* magazine as one of the most rapidly growing and successful small businesses in the United States. In one of our TIGERS trainings, Prafke discovered it was increasingly important for her employees to have a working understanding and appreciation for one another's differences. She viewed these differences as dynamic opportunities for employee career growth, leadership development, and Humanix business success. She used the strengths of their collective differences for problem solving and conflict resolution. She also used her awareness of individual employee's strengths for strategic marketing advantage.

For example, I attended a Personnel Managers Association luncheon where I met one of Humanix's clerical support people. Although she was not directly involved in business recruitment for Humanix, she had been invited to attend the luncheon in recognition for her good work and service.

As personnel managers introduced themselves, one guest told us she was a new member of the community. She also mentioned her prior management experience and her desire to find new employment. Although personnel recruiters from numerous companies attended this meeting, the Humanix secretary took a genuine interest in the newcomer and began to ask her questions.

During the following month's meeting, the guest once again introduced herself. Only this time she reported that she had taken a temporary management position through Humanix and would be substituting for an employee who was home on medical leave for a number of months. Although the Humanix secretary lacked job placement authority, her gregarious nature and willingness to help created an opportunity that other qualified job placement personnel had missed.

The Third Culture

A team's contribution is greater than the sum of its parts as shown in the interdependence equation, $1 + 1 > 2$. This is because people choose goals that complement commonly held agreements, principles, purposes, and intent. The common ground, when based on quality and the sound uplifting principles embodied in TIGERS, influences interpersonal respect, trust, genuineness, empathy, and success in implementing group goals.

Another characteristic of the $1 + 1 > 2$ equation is the emergence of a third culture. Founded upon education and sound communication principles, it embraces the following ideas: *As people teach each other about themselves, interdependent aware-ness evolves. By integrating knowledge of one another, a new invisible third culture emerges that is always changing.* When people emotionally, experientially, and holistically grow, the in-visible culture also changes. It is fed by the diversity each person brings to the relationship. The third culture changes based on the quality of information shared and understanding acquired. It is the team's essence.

The third culture is best observed in terms of energy. It is similar to kinetic energy, which is energy in motion. The math-ematical equation for kinetic energy is $\frac{MV^2}{2}$. The energy of a body that results from its motion is equal to half the product of its mass and the square of its velocity.

For example, the energy of the team is the cohesive chemis-try, synergy, and life force of the third culture. Although it encompasses a separate identity from each team member, it is composed of the energy each person contributes to the team. Its motion is based on the reality that people are different and circumstances change.

The mass portion relates to the weight of understanding achieved when people educate one another about new work procedures, personal changes, experiences, thoughts, feelings, and closely-held, nonnegotiable values. It is a challenging aspect of the equation because sharing personal vulnerabilities is some-times necessary. It takes a very trusting, strong, and self-assured person to share personal weaknesses with others. For this rea-son, people schooled in relationship awareness and emotional team management are valuable resources for long-term team maintenance.

The velocity portion of the equation represents the rate at which expressed changes are understood, accepted, and inte-grated. In our model, however, velocity is not squared but is multiplied to an unnamed power. This is because relationship enrichment involves an empathetic and sometimes exponential process. For example, people must often accept one another on faith. Also, when one person understands and integrates another person's experiences, thoughts, and feelings, it can alter the way the first person perceives the world. Repeated integration is therefore enriched by interpersonal education and ever-increasing awareness.

The division of the product by two represents the effect of conflict on relationships. If integration and increased understanding emerge from conflict, then the relationship aspect of the equation increases. If the opposite holds true, then the changing team life force is reduced. Our revised equation looks something like this:

$$\text{3rd Culture (Relationship)} = \frac{\text{Understanding} \times \text{Rate of Integration}^n}{\text{Conflict}}$$

where n represents an unnamed multiplier.

When conflict arises and is not resolved and understanding is not achieved, the net result is reduced team life force. This is why in some group endeavors, the net performance is lower than if one capable person had done the work alone. On the other hand, when a team communicates well, cares about what it is doing, and works to resolve conflict through understanding and acceptance, the individual relationships build and improve.

Furthermore, opportunities might also evolve out of the problem-solving and relationship-building process. This is especially true when people create synthesis from adversarial positions.

For example, synthesis led to the nuclear disarmament between the United States and the former Soviet Union. The realization that an escalating arms race could only lead to global disaster and dwindling financial reserves created the window of opportunity for the former Soviet Union and the United States to quit competing. The recognition introduced a new balance of power and the realization that if one party to a dispute withdraws, the other will eventually have to as well or bear the consequences of global disapproval.

Since the third culture (relationship) is always changing, people leaving and joining a team influence its dynamic. However, teams hold together when the quality of interpersonal communication, interpersonal understanding, respect, and reverence remain high.

Furthermore, resistance between people lessens when people seek to expand into a greater encompassing culture. The education and group learning process allows for the emergence of a third culture that is greater than its parts. A crucial aspect of the $1 + 1 > 2$ equation, however, is that people exhibit high levels of self-awareness in order to diagnose and claim responsibility for their own limitations.

What Happens If Everyone Is the Same?

Remember that by their nature, people are different. People think differently. They also have different life experiences. But this does not mean that one person is better than another. It simply means they are different. By building upon the strengths of their differences, a group's outcomes often surpass the potential of each person alone.

A strong group is often made up of a balance of Doers, Analyzers, and Relationship-oriented people. However, a team forged from people with similar strengths or experiences has the potential for blind spots in working through a problem. When too many members approach a problem in the same way, groupthink may emerge.

Groupthink is a term coined by I.L. Janis in a 1977 book *Decision Making.* Janis observed that some highly cohesive groups tended to develop and implement projects that missed the target or were inappropriate. This occurred because team members made decisions quickly, without thoroughly evaluating the alternatives. Some members avoided confronting the majority because dissension was not tolerated. They felt they had to sensor themselves or others would apply social pressure through gossip and shunning. Groupthink also involves stereotypes and illusions that affect good decision making. For example, team members may believe they are invulnerable and bolster themselves against "outsiders." An *us* and *them* division develops, and the team loses the benefit of diverse opinions and experience. In spite of the dysfunction, the team perpetuates a harmonious facade by avoiding open disagreement.

When full-blown groupthink is in progress, team members react negatively to new or challenging information. They develop an arrogance that devalues critical thinking and questioning. This is true even though the undiscussed information may be valid and important. The result on the third culture is a plunging group intelligence.

One of the most recent public discussions involving groupthink addressed the Republican push to repeal Affirmative Action, which was put into place to correct unfair and discriminatory hiring practices by Anglo-European males against minorities and women. Over the past twenty years, legislated career strides have been made by minorities and women.

Currently the climate has shifted to where it is more difficult for Anglo-European males to compete for jobs. The question now arises whether job discrimination in any form is ethical and justified.

Many women and minorities assert that without job hiring protection, their career opportunities would be jeopardized. Anglo-European males, however, argue that people should be hired on their merit. Has the justification for Affirmative Action run its course?

In March 1995, the report of a three-year study commissioned by the Bush administration stated that white males occupy 97 percent of Fortune 1,000 senior management positions. They also reported that only 5 percent of the top managers at Fortune 2,000 industrial and service companies are women. However, 66 percent of the overall population and 57 percent of the workforce is minority or a female or both. Clearly groupthink involves certain kinds of illusions and stereotypes that interfere with effective decision making.

Groupthink is an unfortunate team pitfall. One way to avoid it is to build diversity into the process by establishing a problem-solving procedure designed to evaluate numerous alternatives. Another possibility is for team members to analyze new information apart from the team to form individual opinions before discussion. A third way to avoid groupthink is to encourage critical thinking.

Keep in mind, too, that team member diversity increases the potential for team conflict. This is especially true during predictable stages of team growth. The potential for conflict also increases when people are dependent upon events outside themselves for harmony and self-esteem. However, interpersonal sensitivities can be emotionally managed, brought to light, and discussed. It is a matter of proactive education resulting in trust and interdependence building.

One executive who has worked hard to employ critical thinking and questioning to deflect groupthink is Barclay Kingel, owner of Fresh Foods Corporation of America, also known as Cyrus O'Leary's wholesale pies. Well read in effective management practices, Kingel developed an employee survey to evaluate supervisors.

However, his manufacturing supervisor's first reaction to the survey was negative. The supervisor, who had been recruited from Nabisco Corporation, felt the survey's use was potentially dangerous. His past experience with employee surveys had resulted in firings. He was able to present his past experience within a helpful context to broaden Kingel's perspective.

Drawing on his belief that a quality-based company nurtures a culture composed of good checks and balances, Kingel saw critical evaluation as a tool to talk about the future and ongoing success of the company. Through his managing supervisor's feedback, Kingel's initial idea to develop employee surveys was improved to address the true question: How can the company acquire valuable feedback from hourly employees on the production floor? The evaluation process lead to the invention of a feedback system addressing Cyrus O'Leary's unique and progressive needs.

In order to be intellectually, physically, and emotionally interdependent, people must retain their own identities, commit to the group, and commit to personal growth and wholeness. Furthermore, since a group is a collection of individuals and an organization is a collection of groups, organizational success hinges on both work quality and interpersonal cooperation.

Various studies conclude that interdependence and the necessary cooperation to accomplish work are the main reasons for team development. In essence then, teams require a collective task, and their success is based on the technical, interpersonal, and emotional investment each team member contributes to the whole.

My Response to the Question

Recall the question raised by the public education union member: "Why do I have to give up who I am in order to make our meetings work?" The answer is, you don't. It is not ethical to require people to change who they *are* to fit into a group. Likewise, when people confuse who they are with their behavior, they will often hold on dearly to old habits and practices.

Nor is it ethical to ask people to breech alignment between their work and personal values, a practice common in competitive-based organizations. However, if in honest self-reflection, team members acknowledge that group success is suffering because of their personal actions, is it ethical to continue their behavior?

Self-awareness and personal responsibility are necessary when contemplating the question, "Is this group right for me?" Turning this question around and projecting it outward, the question becomes, "Am I right for this group?" Once people are aware of their basic emotional and mental qualities, they can make an effort to assess their strengths and weaknesses.

Marjory Kelly, editor and founder of *Business Ethics* magazine wrote: "A new kind of person [is] coming into power. A powerful person, but one who wields power with care. A successful person, but for whom success isn't everything. That special person who strives to live and work in responsible ways. Who wants to live comfortably, but never carelessly. Who wants to create businesses that are healthy places to work." It is this type of person who is also willing to leap from the competitive paradigm to an interdependent one requiring self-reflection and accountability: a person who has crossed the chasm between self-interest and a global perspective. A person with the good sense of a goose.

Although one could argue that Reverend Fast's speech depicts a homogenous culture, I've seen different. Specifically, one summer morning I was walking around Manito Pond in Spokane, Washington. I watched a heart-touching example of care and interdependence in action.

A goose was guarding and supporting an ailing duck. The duck appeared to have a damaged wing and was limping. As companion, the goose stayed close by the duck's side and allowed the duck to eat some bread tossed by sympathetic people. The goose ate nothing until the duck had eaten its fill. It also stood between the duck and people who ventured too close. It would charge and beat its wings to ward them off. The goose had extended its instincts beyond those of like kind.

Do new paradigms require personal and cultural change? Sure. They also require fresh discernment. And, as organizations mature from competitive and independent practices to collaborative and interdependent procedures, new skills, relationships, and thinking are required.

Interdependence calls for an appreciation of diversity, cooperation, respect, reverence, accountability, and self-reflection. Therefore, a diligent desire to improve one's personal effectiveness both in work and in interpersonal relationship is an *expectation* of the interdependent paradigm.

And, although personal growth is one benefit derived from the process, adaptability in radically changing times is another. If interdependence brings about greater understanding between people and respect for differences, then site-based counsels, healthy companies, productive work teams, and communities will also benefit from increased success, a success where people assert the work was worth it and they'd do it again.

Wendy Nomathemba Luhabe graduated with a Bachelor of Commerce in 1981, after which she pursued a career in marketing, working in South Africa, Germany, and the U.S. In 1992, she left the profession to open a practice in human resources development and management, working to realign archaic human resources practices with a changing marketplace.

In 1992, she became the youngest black woman to become a director in a Johannesburg Stock Exchange listed company. In 1994, Luhabe pioneered the participation of women in the economy. The portfolio includes investments in the telecommunications, media services, and fast-moving consumer goods industries.

In 1997, Luhabe was nominated by the World Economic Forum to join the growing population of Global Leaders for Tomorrow.

6

Bridging the Gap

Wendy Nomathemba Luhabe

Bridging the Gap is the name we chose to describe the work we do in our company, Human Resources Renaissance. It seems appropriate that I should use the seame name as my theme, to share with you areas of human interaction that unequivocally stand in the way of our embracing and respecting diversity. My observations, both in my career development experience and as a practitioner in the experiential application of human resources systems, have convinced me that what we experience in the workplace is a consequence of our poor preparedness for life as a diverse system. So the areas to which I want to draw your attention relate to the gaps in our perceptions; how we understand each other and the world; the balance of power and how we use that power to keep others marginalized; our ability to take responsibility for both our failures and achievements; and the knowledge that provides us with the tools to cope and make something of our lives. Finally, I want to touch on the basic human values such as honesty, compassion, forgiveness, fairness, and respect, which make it possible for us to honor each other and the potential waiting to blossom, if only someone gives it a chance.

Regrettably, we have compartmentalized our lives into home, work, education, and other places we go to. The reality is these places are not separate; they overlap each other and influence one another constantly. Our limitation seems to be an inability to use the family structure, our work lives, church, educational, or recreational lives to add value to each other.

Each institution has a critical role to play, but that role can only be maximized if we weave a thread through all of them. We must see life as a system of interrelationships between the people who inhabit that system and the institutions that hold the systems of life together. I cannot imagine a life without family, work, education, or the many other resources that are essential for our development.

Let me emphasize, however, that the family structure provides the soul of existence. If family life breaks down, as it has in South Africa, we experience the decay of values and morals. The family is what we are born into; it is the structure that prepares us for life by providing us with food, education, shelter, wisdom, and direction. If these functions are not fulfilled adequately, we create a society that is incapable of triumphing.

Diversity

Diversity is absolutely fundamental in preparing society to accept and embrace change in a turbulent and uncertain world. The ability to embrace and respect diverse viewpoints and cultures is a competence that we in South Africa do not have as a society. Therefore, the question is what do we have to learn as a society to be able to develop the ability to embrace a viewpoint, a behavior, and a culture that is unfamiliar, different, unusual, strange, distasteful, and all the descriptions that enter our minds when we are judgmental? I shall discuss what would allow us to acknowledge that we lack the ability and respect in the first place, and what would give us the courage to develop this new ability without any fear of being changed or giving up our own viewpoint, reality, and culture or losing our identity, but simply learning to coexist with others in the same way that nature seems to manage.

Five years ago, I left what is regarded as the hard area of commerce to work in the so-called soft area of human resources. Human resources is the only profession in the economy that gives us an opportunity, on a daily basis, to live and practice the profession we have chosen in the way that we deal with each other and develop relationships, interact with each other, see each other, and honor each other. It is the only field in commerce that reminds us of our humanity. Let me share with you my own understanding of diversity, as I have no doubt that there are many versions, which may be part of the problem.

If we do not define what we mean and understand, we create confusion and room for society to resist what could fundamentally be a sustainable solution to human conflict, instability, and dysfunction in the world. So, my understanding of diversity is the following: Diversity is a new culture of human behavior that honors people where they are, with what they know, how they acquired this knowledge, and how they apply it. This could be different for each person. Fundamentally, diversity changes people from machines and objects, numbers, and statistics, into people who have minds and hearts to make a difference in the world, to play their simple but important parts in the acts of living and creating. My understanding submits that we are all at different stations in life. We know different things, have different experiences and capabilities, respond differently to what we see, hear, and feel. God intended us to be this way. The conspiracy that only a particular way is acceptable and therefore must be dominant is an indictment of what God intended us to achieve with each of our lives. This reminds me of a story that Angeles Arrien tells in her workshops: When we make a transition from this life, God conducts an interview about our lifetime, and there is only one question that He asks us. "Wendy, I gave you everything you needed, my breath to sustain you through life, a mind, a heart, a body and soul. Tell me, why were you not Wendy whilst you lived?"

I have always found this story a profound reminder of what I am here to do and similarly, what others are here to do. I have a responsibility to inspire those I come into contact with to blossom. If I meet them as a blossom, I have a responsibility to allow them to go to become fruit.

So I submit that diversity may be all we need to practice in order to evolve a new context and a new coherent world map for society. I prefer to call it a coherent world map because I recognize that we each have our individual maps—family maps, race maps, gender maps, cultural maps, and many others—that we hold on to for dear life. What we need to do is identify the common elements in each of these maps, so we can create a coherent world map without throwing away all the others we have been using and have come to depend upon. It's possible that we may find the new world map a lot more precise and meaningful in enabling us to cope with each other and the growing uncertainty around us. In my experience and in the work that I do, it has become quite clear that what inhibits us from embracing the unknown are the maps that we carry in our minds. And because we are inhibited, we inhibit others.

I have come to understand that the mind is a survival and exploitation tool; it knows only how to be rational, judgmental, manipulative, calculating, and everything else we need to survive in a ruthless world. It does not know how to be compassionate, understanding, and patient.

The challenge therefore is for us to learn to interact with our hearts, a tool more disposed to expansiveness, openness, sincerity, and truth. The heart does not have a map; it does not know how to judge. It simply maintains our life force and deep compassion. This is why I propose that humanity must, as a matter of priority, learn how to be in relationship with itself. We have to simply go back to basics and learn how to be in relationship using the heart as a bridge. The word *heart* contains many profound words that enable us to be in relationship with each other.

- hear—if I can't hear you, I can't be in relationship with you. Most of us are deaf. We simply cannot hear or do not want to hear.

- art—being in relationship is an art. We create something through our interaction; our relationship tells a story. The meaning changes from moment to moment.

- ear—the ear represents receptivity and plays an important role in receiving what others have to offer and share as a gift, but it can also protect us if what is offered is harmful.

The way to our heart is through our ears. If someone says, "I love you," I hear that with my ears before my heart is evoked. Therefore, the ear is a vital communication bridge between people. Listening displays a deep respect for others. Perhaps we must learn to be poets—in that way it would be easier to create a workplace that has a human conscience.

What Are the Gaps?

Perception

I was watching and listening to a physicist, a politician, and a poet having a dialogue in the documentary movie "Mindwalk," based on Fritjof Capra's book *The Turning Point*. The speakers raised many issues that have a lot of relevance regarding working together. First, the poet said, "The stone speaks and I am silent." Can you imagine the depth and breadth of that thought? It could be suggesting that the language of the heart is what we have to learn. Next, the speakers talked about a crisis of perception as being the real reason for the incoherence in the world. Then a thought occurred to me: If the way we perceive is really causing conflict and dysfunction in the world, perhaps diversity can bridge the perception gap that exists in our realities. The gap in our perceptions is making it impossible for us to be in relationship with each other, to really connect with each other in the way that we seem to with animals, for example, or with nature.

Perhaps, in a strange way, it is convenient for us to maintain this gap in our perceptions. This way we are under no pressure to discover a new way of understanding the world and the diverse people that are its citizens. The operative idea here is *fear of discovery*. This could be a fear that after so many years of dehumanizing others, we may discover that they are, after all, human, just as we are.

Recognizing this would require us to break down the walls we have been building and confront our shame and guilt, which of course we don't really want to acknowledge. It's too much hard work, so we would rather carry the burden than be set free.

This is why I maintain that diversity is a way to bridge the many gaps that we experience. The perception gap is really the most fundamental, as it shapes each of our realities in the most powerful way. Perceptions keep us apart and isolated, they force us to deny others what we know is important to maintain humanity and personal dignity in ourselves and in others.

Power

There is an imbalance of power in the world—in the way we understand the world and each other, in the knowledge and experiences we hold—that keeps the majority marginalized and dependent on a system that continues to squeeze them rather than expand to accommodate them. Many of us are helpless and have long since disposed of our personal power. As a result, the few that have stolen the power use it to exploit others, not to liberate. Power was meant to liberate individuals to exercise choices in their lives, to question, to grow and take responsibility for their own existence. However, we find ourselves incapable because our power is diminished from the moment we are born.

By the time we make a transition to the next life, we have absolutely nothing left but a void. It seems to me that diversity can restore this loss of power, particularly if we use one another as bridges. I observe in South Africa, for example, what happens when a society has been systematically denied access to power.

For many of us it remains difficult to make decisions, to provide leadership, to take a stand, and to maintain integrity for ourselves and for others who look to us for direction and resilience. So what we end up doing is pulling each other down. We may not even realize that this is what we are doing because the behavior has become deeply internalized.

The very structure of society is designed to divide and rule. Nowhere is the consequence of that more evident than in South Africa. We used the mind so effectively here as a tool to break people down, ultimately to nothing. The system succeeded in making us invisible and insignificant. Diversity can provide a bridge for us to become whole again, to claim our human consciousness and dignity, to honor and embrace the gaps that have created so much fragmentation and hemorrhaging that it has become unbearable. We need to create a culture that self-organizes and transcends. That ability has to do with power and where the ability to exercise power rests in society.

Responsibility

As we grow up, we are not allowed to think, make decisions, or make choices. We live a protected life that is punctuated with, "Don't do that," "No," and "You can't." Our parents regard us so often as incapable that in the end we believe it. The tragedy is we assume that everyone else is also incapable. Learning to be responsible offers us the ability to treat the causes rather than the symptoms of what doesn't work in the world as a gift for humanity to be fully prepared to function in the twenty-first century.

The way we are brought up does not prepare us equally for life. Some of us go through tertiary education in a daze; we sleepwalk through it and perhaps never wake up for fear of living. Some of us study what our friends want to study or what our parents want us to study, or what is the easiest.

So we perpetuate a pattern in our lives where we do nothing for ourselves and everything we can for everyone else, while we complain that the world will not devote itself to making us happy. No wonder the only question that God asks us is, "Wendy! Why weren't you Wendy whilst you were alive?" Well, because it is damn difficult when I am not taught to take responsibility for my life, to make my own choices and live with their consequences, to fail and try and try again, to take risks so I can stretch my abilities and discover new possibilities—to really find out in the most extraordinary way that I can be a gift to the world. Parents live their unfulfilled lives through their children; they attempt to correct their failures through their children. As a result, children who are born into each generation never live their own lives. All we should be required to do is to prepare children to take full responsibility for their lives. We should inspire them to be independent, to be whole human beings, and with that they will know what do to, how to live, and how to be creative instead of resentful and constricted by the way we have brought them up. Life's a puzzle and each one of us holds a piece. That piece is our full expression, the opportunity to fulfill our human potential, the possibility to create something that takes humanity to the next level of evolution. So we must resist the mechanistic way of living. We are not machines; we can accomplish so much more if we build bridges for each other, if we allow our interconnectedness to guide us toward new and sustainable solutions. That commitment requires each one of us to take responsibility.

Knowledge

It is often said in South Africa that if you want to hide something from black people, put it in a book. At first I thought, *how ridiculous*. But then I sat on the thought for a while and found myself agreeing. The reality is that reading and writing is something African people have developed recently. Traditionally, we are an oral people, and this is the best way to teach us anything. Tell us a story and you will catch our imagination. This could also be the reason that we do not document as much as other cultures. We did not write, therefore it doesn't occur to us to read. We spoke and through that developed an ability to listen. This is not a deficiency. But when we live in a society that conveys knowledge in a mechanistic way, in a written format, we do not learn very well, we do not integrate the knowledge and apply it in the same way as other cultures. To say we are stupid or lazy is simply an inability to imagine that different cultures learn differently and apply their knowledge differently.

The practice of embracing diversity in our daily lives would allow us to begin to understand that and revise our expectations toward an attitude that reaches toward the success of others instead of the failures. If I start from a position that wants you to succeed, I will be more supportive, compassionate, and respectful. If I start from a place that assumes you will fail, I will naturally, knowingly or not, sabotage you, undermine you, be hostile and disrespectful. We have insufficient, and in most cases incorrect, information to relate to the world effectively.

What we learned at school, at home, and from our environment, which is different for every culture, is insufficient for us to resist being judgmental and cynical. It happens automatically, before we can even notice that we are being judgmental. That is the tragedy. We need others to give us more information so that ultimately we hold a complete and clear picture of how the world functions and how each of the segments fit in.

Values

Working together is a value that should start at home between mothers and fathers, husbands and wives, children and parents, brothers and sisters, sisters and sisters, brothers and brothers, fathers and daughters, mothers and sons. Perhaps it is not possible to learn to work together if it is not a value we bring with us from home. Whatever we want to create in society manifests itself at home first, then in the community and beyond. Working together as a family allows us the freedom to practice with diversity in a safe environment, at home.

It would probably eliminate most of the dysfunctional behaviors that have become the norm because we would learn to interact in a way that is expansive. We would use each other as instruments for accessing a greater understanding of what is really created when people interact within the framework of values. The family is most likely the ultimate structure that God uses to empower humanity. But we have broken that fabric. Our family structure lacks the values and the discipline to protect truth. The two go hand in hand. I must be disciplined to observe human values, particularly for my health, relationships, and decisions, but all three areas have completely broken down in society. We see too many diseases and divorces, too much indecision and poor leadership. It is therefore possible that diversity is an invitation for the family structure to rethink its role in a rapidly changing world. Mother Teresa once said, "We are all instruments of God, and however imperfect we are, God writes through us."

If we discard those who are imperfect in society, imagine

how much is lost, and imagine the pressure this creates on those who are perfect.

Conclusion

Embracing diversity is not a favor to others who are different from ourselves, it is a favor to ourselves, as it gives us permission to grow. Its practice allows us to see that we are not free, and in that discovery we dispose of our fear of others, the new and unknown. Hopefully we will realize that we have a choice to risk living, touching someone, or following our dream. I've always had dreams, followed them, and ultimately realized them. Then I find new ones to take me to the next step. Life is about taking a step at a time, the way we started when we learned to walk. If we walk too fast, we may fall. If we take the wrong step, we may fall. The challenge is to get up and continue on our path, which can only be walked by us and no one else. It is along that path that our gifts are hidden in the relationships we encounter, the goals we define for ourselves, and the wisdom that we develop.

Perhaps the major virtue of diversity is that it allows each one of us to expand our definition of reality. As we mature, we perceive more broadly, we empower ourselves to follow our life purpose, we acquire new knowledge so that our range of understanding is broadened, we learn to take responsibility for ourselves and our progress in the world to bridge all of these gaps, we honor basic human values in a way that is contextualized in the principles of diversity. This will ultimately lead us to the transformation of society, more out of commitment than obligation.

Marilyn Hill Harper, M.D. (left), professor of anesthesia, University of California, San Francisco has been on the medical school faculty since 1972. She received her undergraduate degree from Talladega College, medical degree from Howard University, and completed her anesthesia residency and cardiac anesthesia fellowship at the University of Iowa. She is co-author of *Wearing Purple*, a collection of letters that celebrate the process of working in circles and emphasize the value of collaborative work.

Wendy S. Appel, M.A. (right), , is an organization development specialist and a cultural anthropologist. She currently works in this capacity at Kaiser Permanente doing team building, leadership coaching, conflict resolution, communication skills development, and meeting facilitation. Previously, Appel spent 11 years working in the high tech industry in product development and as an account executive. Her personal commitment is to catalyze people's collective wisdom inservice of self, community, and the Earth.

7

Living and Loving in a Diverse World

Marilyn Hill Harper and Wendy S. Appel

"Assumptions formed from the past,
when unchecked, will create the future."
—*Patrick O'Neill*

The following conversation between Marilyn Hill Harper, M.D., African American, anesthesiologist, mother, and writer, and Wendy S. Appel, M.A., Jewish, cultural anthropologist, and consultant, was prompted by the above quote, which was central to our discussion.

MH: I think most readers have at least a passing interest in our uniquely diverse American population. Whether the mix is in the workplace or among their customers or clients, the issues surrounding diversity are affecting every business. I see the challenge as how to join together diverse ideas, perspectives, and points of view in a way that will foster maximum productivity and success. This last statement brings into focus the problem that I think permeates many discussions about diversity. Are we all talking about the same thing? Do we have the same definitions of diversity? What is success? For the purpose of this dialogue, I define diversity as various ethnicities, the nondominant gender, and all the possible combinations of creed, national origin, management style, sexual orientation, and points of view.

I choose to define success as a condition that encourages all members of an organization to maximize their potential, allows creative use of members' abilities, and produces a satisfactory monetary return while actively responding to community and environmental concerns. I think the primary tools for success are respect and loving kindness. I see the primary barrier to success with diversity as assumptions made about non-dominant groups as well as assumptions about how our institutions work.

WA: I find that diversity exists in all shapes, sizes, behaviors, and colors and is a powerful influence on connecting with others or in creating distance. Each of us is a unique individual nowhere else replicated on this Earth. I believe that our uniqueness resides in our souls. Whenever our individuality, our diversity, is denied, there is loss of soul. When we are denied our ability to contribute what we alone bring into this world, there is wounding. We need to know that we can fully be ourselves and still belong.

Recently, I came to the conclusion that social class and hierarchical distinctions in organizations have an enormous amount of influence on prejudice that can transcend ethnic difference. A recent example was given to me by an organizational consultant. A company called on this consultant to assess its situation because it thought it had ethnic diversity problems. What he found was that tension and resentment emanated from something totally unanticipated. The company had carpeting for the executive and management offices, linoleum for the staff, and cement and no air conditioning or insulation for the workers on the assembly line, who were also put in a separate warehouse space. The staff and warehouse employees delineated coworkers by "carpet," "linoleum," or "cement," which created class inequities, separation, and resentment within the organization. Those working on cement were standing on their feet all day, chilled in winter, and sweating in the summer. The hierarchy was visible through cultural symbols that also had implications for working conditions.

Just to go back to what you were saying about assumptions,

a recent personal example happened when I was at a Special Olympics event handing out awards. One of the other volunteers was a man in his mid-50s. He was wearing a baseball cap with a Promise Keepers insignia on the front. I mentally put him in a box with all sorts of attributes based on what I have read about the group and decided that he was part of the Christian Right movement, anti-Semitic, anti–African-American, and so on.

However, I couldn't help thinking about the fact that he had given up his Saturday to volunteer. Then, the anthropologist in me took over. I suspended my assumptions about who I thought he was by approaching him from a place of inquiry and curiosity rather than thinking I knew the type of person he was based on his hat. I asked if he was a member of the Promise Keepers, what the group was about, and what he got out of the group. It turned into a very interesting conversation, and he wasn't at all what I had imagined. His search for community, growth, recovery from addiction, and loss had led him to this group in which he was managing to find some solace. I found him sensitive, thoughtful, and desirous of being a more happy and healthy person. This doesn't mean that he didn't have prejudices; it just means that I was able to see a more inclusive picture of him.

This was an incredible lesson for me about what a disservice it is to make assumptions about people based on nothing other than their affiliation with a particular group. It completely denies a person's individuality and robs me of the ability to know and learn from someone I might have otherwise discarded.

MH: I've learned one way to check out assumptions through my experience of working closely with three other women. Our decisions are made by talking about each issue and listening to our different points of view. Various plans are discussed until we fashion one from many ideas. The result is a plan that all of us can embrace and work to implement. The process can sometimes be tedious and certainly requires both patience and respect for each point of view.

WA: Having participated in a similar process, which I understand is derived from a Native American "council process," I have found that the idea is for each person to listen fully without a particular agenda. This provides an opportunity for exploring our assumptions. In ordinary conversations, these assumptions, which can be deeply hidden from ourselves and others, can shape how we react and create blocks from attentive listening. The more we think our deeply held assumptions and values are threatened, the less likely we are to listen to other points of view.

Being categorized can also come with advantages. It is important to look at the unearned privileges that come along with certain backgrounds, abilities, skin colors, styles, and so forth. When we are aware of our own privileges, it helps to be more empathetic and solicitous of others.

MH: Do you think there are populations in our culture who have easy access to power, money, and jobs?

WA: Absolutely. One group that has had access to power for hundreds of years is Anglo men. It has been my experience that many of them have a decided privilege in moving easily and freely through this culture and others around the world. This group has the easiest access to money and power. How many of them are aware of those who can't go into a store or certain neighborhoods without being suspected of stealing something or are denied credit because of their skin color?

Along with privilege comes power, and it requires an awareness of, and responsibility for, appropriate use of this power. This means making conscious decisions about interactions with others and not misusing power over another gender, people who are of a different socioeconomic class, and so on. Misuse of power can take the form of decision making without taking others into consideration or closing out other voices from having a say in the decision-making process. Some examples I've seen are creating toxic waste dumps in low-income neighborhoods, building sound walls on freeways in wealthy suburban areas and not in low income neighborhoods, not promoting women or minorities to management positions. There are also many other examples.

Ways to avert some of this is to be inclusive in decision making and to listen and take into consideration the voices of all who would be affected by a decision. This is what I see as a component of sharing power. However, inclusion takes time. Over the long term, the benefits to the organization are tremendous. There will be employee buy-in to the decisions, increased job satisfaction, shared responsibility, and increased productivity.

MH: In most institutions, people in power used it to surround themselves with like people. The top positions have been primarily White and male, and the situation perpetuates itself. I think people are more comfortable with those who are most like themselves and see no particular reason to change. The motivation for change to include diverse populations did not come from within our institutions. I think that's how affirmative action came into being. Had women, African Americans, Hispanics, and others been recruited all along, the artificial affirmative action system would not have been necessary.

Affirmative action was designed to ensure entry into schools and job markets that had been closed to women and all people of color. The idealistic outcome imagined a smooth incorporation of those historically excluded groups. That view also imagined recognition of the talents the new groups had to offer. Instead, voices long silenced started speaking but still were not heard. The myth of merit was quickly dispelled as the skills and talents rewarded were those that came in the package most favored by those in power. No attention was given to the process of uncoupling well-established stereotypical opinion from evaluating actual performance of the newcomers. As a result women and people of color were often considered "affirmative action hires," which translated to less worthy and automatically devalued their contributions. Any person whose talent could not be ignored or who was successful in spite of the barriers was considered "exceptional" rather than a true representation of minority group abilities. We have now arrived at a time when the glass ceiling is firmly in place, traditionally oppressed groups still experience discrimination, and the affirmative action policies designed to provide opportunity are under attack.

WA: Inequities are institutionalized in our organizations. They are embedded in our systems, and until each of us is willing to be self-reflective about our contributions to these inequities, the prejudices (prejudging others based on some criteria) that each of us holds, and the power earned and unearned that we have, no amount of diversity training is going to bring forth the synergistic values, benefits, and opportunities of harnessing this diversity. The organization must focus on the messages, subtle and not so subtle, that are sent within it about what type of people are valued and who is not as valued, and whose voices are silenced and whose are heard.

Many people are under the assumption that we all have equal opportunity for success, and through hard work, intelligence, and perseverance we can "get ahead," completely rejecting the notion that factors of gender, age, or skin color, give us unearned power and opportunities to gain a competitive advantage. I think that when this assumption is held, there can be a misuse of power, intentionally or intentionally. Unearned privilege sets up a power imbalance, adversarial relationships, separation, blame, and "White man's guilt." Holding that power hurts you as a human being and hurts the organization. The ability to harness the inherent value of diversity to an organization can only come about by the willingness of the organization and its employees to be self-reflective.

MH: That's a very important point that you're making. I was working on a committee composed entirely of women from different backgrounds. This included their ethnicity, the work they did, and their sexual orientation. Most were middle class at that time, but many were raised in very poor areas. Everybody was working very well together for a while, then the committee started falling apart. We went through a whole process to find out what the problem was, and it turned out that, although cultural background played a small part, the real problem lay in the big division between those who were action-oriented people and those who were process-oriented people.

The process people perceived the action-oriented people as taking over the committee because they were fast decision makers. The process-oriented people tended to be a little shyer, a little quieter, and needed more discussion. It was very interesting how the issue of diversity in that case turned out to be entirely one of problem-solving styles and of action style, and much less one of ethnicity or lifestyle. Initially, people in the group thought there might have been some racial issues involved. However, with the help of a facilitator, we found out it had more to do with personality styles. I found it fascinating that in any situation where you have a diverse group of people, it's important not to make an assumption about what is causing the difficulty. It may not be what you expect it to be all. As an African American, I am careful not to assume all difficult interactions are racially based.

Each person has inherent value and deserves respect. By denigrating a particular group, you are devaluing each member of that group. The effect may be to offend someone unintentionally. The experience you and I had together at the Multicultural Women's Camp is a good example of this.

The incident had to do with a woman who was telling a long and very funny story about how she was treated after an automobile accident. She described how health care professionals dealt with her in the emergency room

WA: She was a professional stand-up comic, wasn't she?

MH: I think so. She made it a very interesting and amusing story. It was ironic because you and I had gone to this diversity camp and were prepared to deal with race issues around Jewishness and Blackness. Suddenly, there we were listening to this woman tell a very vicious but very funny story about doctors and nurses.

She was totally unaware that I was an anesthesiologist. As her story progressed, I became more and more insulted by her routine and felt she was being very unfair to the people who were taking care of her in the emergency room. Her object was not to tell a balanced story, but to tell a funny story, and she was doing that very well. It was an interesting experience for me to be invisible. All my life I have dealt with insults and prejudice about my Blackness, which has been right out there and obvious. In that situation, she had no way of knowing I was insulted, and I didn't say anything.

WA: How did it feel for you to be invisible, as opposed to being an African American woman, two things you could not hide?

MH: At first I felt incredulous. How could she go on like that with me sitting there? Then I realized that she didn't know. I was furious with her and her story. I was so angry I didn't trust myself to speak. I was also angry at myself for not confronting her at the time. On many levels I was uncertain about what to do. What I did was to think about it and decide to deal with it later. My feelings went from surprise at the story, through being embarrassed that my colleagues could behave the way she described, to a fierce desire to defend the health care providers, and ended with anger at her unfair judgment of them.

When we talked about the incident later, you were concerned about whether you should have spoken up for me. This actually opened up an interesting dialogue. We discussed what it's like to be invisible and what it means to be allies for each other and how much responsibility each of us should carry for someone else. The next day I told her I was a doctor, and she was apologetic and very sorry she had insulted me unknowingly. I think it was a good lesson for the whole group.

WA: She also became aware that the way she told the story was attacking an entire group of people, rather than making it specific to the doctors and nurses involved in her care.

At diversity camp the phrase "being an ally" got bandied about, and I didn't really know what it meant. When she performed the comedy routine, I assumed you were upset but didn't know if it was appropriate to speak up for you or not. The next day when you raised the issue in the group, some people were wondering why I didn't speak up for you and criticized me for not being your ally. To this day, I believe you and I handled it in a way that was mutually respectful.

I remember one evening during our class with Angeles Arrien, I learned what being an ally was really like. Someone in our class was describing a project she completed and used the phrase "black talk," as something related to one's inner critic or a negative internal dialog. In that moment, my need to stand up for what I believed in overcame my fear of embarrassing the speaker and of being criticized for being overly sensitive. I felt absolutely compelled to bring it to the group's attention. I was sitting across the circle from you and I could see you were disturbed, but that wasn't why I spoke up. It wasn't about taking care of you. I felt obliged to say something because I thought an injustice was being done. In that moment, both of us understood what it meant to be allies to each other. Prejudice doesn't just hurt the target group, it hurts everyone. When prejudice is let in the door and isn't acknowledged for what it is, it invites other forms of prejudice into the room as well.

MH: It turned out a lot of people were uncomfortable but nobody had the courage to say anything until you did; not even me. It's such a common experience for me to hear people use black as a catch-all for negative, for wrong, or for evil. What you are saying is that being an ally means speaking up when you feel an injustice is being done and not necessarily to defend someone. I think being sensitive to all kinds of injustices and being willing to speak up could help defuse tense situations.

WA: I wouldn't do it to simply take care of you because I think each of us needs to feel the power of standing up for ourselves instead of shrinking from the wounds, intentionally or unintentionally inflicted. If you asked for my help, I would have been there instantly. I would also support you when and if you decided to speak.

MH: Just to change the subject slightly, do you have any idea why diversity is so difficult for most of us?

WA: Perhaps our struggle in accepting diversity, that there can simultaneously be multiple perspectives, is that we have difficulty embracing the diversity that exists within each of us. I am Jewish, of Russian and Austrian heritage, female, heterosexual, an anthropologist, a business woman, middle class, extroverted, athletic, have strong environmental values, decisive and indecisive, strong and soft, vulnerable and powerful, liberal and conservative. I am many things.

Instead, life is more simple when you can put people, events, or issues in a box and label it right or wrong, good or bad. It is the desire to make our world and ourselves knowable and deny the paradoxes that exist that makes living with internal and external diversity uncomfortable.

I saw the movie *Dead Man Walking*. The prisoner who was on death row belonged to a White supremacy group and hated Blacks and Jews because he despised people who he thought were victims. Ultimately he came to understand that he had self-hatred for being a victim. What he rejected about other people was what he feared most about himself. A lot of our dislike about people we think are different from us is that we see something in them that reminds us of part of ourselves that we don't like, don't accept, or don't acknowledge.

We create all sorts of myths about people we think are different from us. We live with these myths and make up stories when we don't have direct contact. That creates separation and can bring about distrust and hate. I believe those are two major factors influencing our lack of tolerance for those people we perceive as different from ourselves. It could be the color of their skin, their beliefs, their religion, or their sexual preference. We immediately assume we won't like them because of one thing, and we end up discarding them entirely.

When parts of ourselves are denied, disavowed, or hated, it is called internalized oppression. Because of all of the anti-Semitism I have experienced, there are times I have been ashamed of being Jewish, or get angry at other Jewish people for fitting certain stereotypes, or don't stand up for myself when someone makes an anti-Semitic remark in conversation, unaware that I am Jewish. You see, "I pass" because I don't have stereotypical Semitic features people associate with being Jewish. From a very young age, I became ashamed of my Jewish heritage because of the negative things I was told directly and indirectly about what it meant to be Jewish from friends, classmates, TV, magazines, and other Jewish people who put themselves down. I began to believe these judgments and deny to myself and others that part of who I am. I would rather blend in than stand out as different. I was afraid to act "too Jewish." By trying to fit in, I have denied my ethnic and spiritual heritage. Slowly I am beginning to reclaim them. I know the challenge for me it to accept myself and to bring all parts of me forward into any situation without denying or aggrandizing who I am.

MH: The impact of business decisions on individual employee well-being or the community as a whole does not appear to be an important issue. This brings me to the issue of spirituality, which appears to be absent from most organizations. The whole thrust of what I believe is that each person should be viewed as a valuable human being because each person is part of the Great Spirit, whether you call it Christ, Buddha, Allah, Mother Earth, the Goddess, the Universe, or God.

WA: When I talk about spirituality, what I refer to is understanding that we are part of the greater whole. That what we do is not in isolation; that we affect other people by our actions or inactions. Everything and everyone is interconnected. We need to think more as a community and less as discrete individual units. Our actions have an impact; and each of us makes a difference.

I believe that the decisions made by legislative bodies and business institutions should be based on this concept in addition to the current profit-driven decisions. This is not making "religious" dogma part of the government and business but rather including in it how we make decisions about what we do in this country.

Gandhi knew that the material world could not be separated from the spiritual world; business could not be separated from the ultimate good of humanity.

MH: I think ethical and ecological values should be part of every single governmental or business decision-making process. The bottom line should not be short-term profit but the impact on the whole ecosystem.

WA: A healthy company should mimic a healthy ecosystem. Without diversity in nature, the earth would shrivel up and die, and so would we. You can always tell a healthy ecosystem because there is diversity in plant and animal life. When you have monocultures, meaning a culture that is just one type of plant, the type of life it supports is very limited. Diverse birds, insects, and animals can no longer survive in that environment; nor can humans. Instead of thumbing our nose at diverse viewpoints, opinions, backgrounds, and people, we need to really honor the value and wisdom that arises from differences.

Living this way asks each of us to continually expand our definition of self, other, and the world. It is inclusive rather than exclusive. In the best of all worlds, the structure and function of an organization would mimic a healthy ecosystem, which knows that it will not thrive without diversity and interdependence.

MH: Part of the problem is that even though this is understood in concept, what frequently happens is that the long term is sacrificed for the short term. The next financial quarter is the longest view, the bottom line at the end of the quarter.

WA: One of the key spiritual values that I hold dear, one that is a part of many Native American cultures, is making decisions with the next seven generations in mind. What are long, long-term consequences of our actions? What kind of world are we leaving for our children, and their children? That is an exemplar of the kind of values that should be brought into the decision-making process in organizations and communities.

MH: This reminds me of something I was going to say earlier about picking out the difference and creating distance because of the difference. When you and I met, it was in a very loving environment. We had interest in the seminar in common or we wouldn't have been there. But our experience of each other as strangers was to look for where we had commonalties. We did that without being told to do it, without it being deliberate; it's just how we speak. Looking for commonality as the initial interchange between strangers would eliminate a lot of the tension when you have diverse people together. I would like to see the intent be to find the commonalties instead of only focusing on difference and making difference wrong. The realization of our interconnectedness would become more important than illusions of separateness.

WA: Marilyn, how do you suggest people begin shifting their focus to include our commonalties in addition to our differences?

MH: One place to start would be to have an intention to interact with love and compassion. It's easier to extend kindness and speak gently to those with whom we feel affection and identification. I suggest our words and actions be kind toward all persons, not just those with whom we have a special affinity.

WA: I would add to what you said by suggesting that we not deny or suppress our anger but rather deliver it with compassion and without judgment and blame. Gandhi taught that truth telling was the best policy, even in politics. It provides the opportunity to solve problems of diversity from the heart.

We can reconcile the power and love that resides within each of us by telling the truth without blaming or judging and by taking responsibility for our contribution to any conflict. We can approach someone with love and compassion once we acknowledge that there is a connection between individuals—we are not separate, and what I do to you I am also doing to myself. One way to establish this connection is to take the time to listen to each other's stories and find the humanity common to each person. Another is to examine the assumptions we may have about another and test out our assumptions instead of acting on them. It's also important to explore our own internalized oppression lest we become oppressors. The last point is to remember that there are multiple ways to believe, live, and love. Each of us has our unique path, and it is important to honor and respect each person's journey. As Rumi said, "There are hundreds of ways to kneel and kiss the ground." These are the ingredients that create opportunities for harnessing the richness of diversity that has the potential to enhance our businesses, relationships, and inner lives.

When we can fully express our individuality without fear of being reproached, we can begin to live in relationship to our communities in ways that will feed the soul of the members and that will honor both the differences and the underlying unity of our lives.

When there are walls of ignorance between people, when we don't know each other's stories, we substitute our own myth about who that person is. When we are operating with only a myth, none of that person's truth will ever be known to us, and we will injure them—mostly without ever meaning to. What assumption did you make because she's a woman? What assumption did you make because he is Black? What myths were built around the employment of the father or the absence of the mother? What story did we tell ourselves in the absence of knowing this person's real Story?

—Paula Lawrence Wehmiller

Suzie Williams is a national speaker and workshop leader on intuition and spiritual development. She is a contributing author to *Intuition at Work: Pathways to Unlimited Possibilities.*

She has a lifelong interest in building and renewing organizational cultures in which team spirit, authentic leadership, and community thrive. Her most recent contribution has been in promoting a cooperative spirit and creating partnerships between the national association and the twenty-nine regional associations in the promotional products industry.

Williams has had fifteen years of middle and senior management experience in the corporate environment, mainly in the areas of government relations, regional relations, and investor relations.

8

Recipes for Synergy

Suzie Williams

The mountains,
I become part of it...
The herbs, the fir tree,
I become part of it...
The morning mists, the clouds,
The gathering waters,
I become part of it...
The wilderness, the dewdrops, the pollen
I become part of it.
—*Navajo Chant*

I've always considered myself lucky to have been raised on a farm in Arkansas. For it was there I learned some of my most valued lessons.

In sharing some of my experiences and insights, I hope I will encourage you to look deeply and touch the source of your true wisdom so we may begin to transcend our wrong actions and honor our diversity. It is my fondest hope that we enter the twenty-first century with a spirit of mutual respect, understanding, and acceptance. If we do, our world will benefit.

Synergy and Diversity Are
Everywhere in Nature

My journey into the miraculous began at a very early age. Nature and farm life provided a kind of spontaneous learning that was the center of my life. My teachers were the animals, the stars, the weather, the plants and, of course, my family. They nurtured me, comforted me, inspired me, and educated me. As a child, I began to understand and value the diversity in all things.

Looking back, I still have a deep appreciation for the harmony of life on the farm. The animals, the plants, and my family all meshed together despite our differences, and an interdependence was created. I realize we were like the bread my mother baked each morning in the kitchen. The eggs, the milk, the flour, the salt, the sugar—all these ingredients sitting on the shelf showed no resemblance to what they would become when blended together.

Synergy and diversity are everywhere in nature. When you plant a garden and tend to farm animals, you become sensitive to seasonal changes. You quickly learn that everything is subject to cyclic laws. The seasons of the year flow into one another with fixed regularity and nature's and animals' sensitivity follow the demands of the seasons. When autumn approaches, all of life that continues to survive begins to adapt to the season. It's magical watching the pelt of an animal thicken in anticipation of winter, as well as watching the bark of a tree thicken to protect itself from the cold. Insects burrow deep inside the trees to hibernate. When spring comes, animals shed their protective coats and the insects return to a life of movement. By observing these miraculous events, one can develop a sincere appreciation and respect for how nature and animals work together. By contemplating the cosmic laws and their effects on life, you can also gain tremendous insight on the value of honoring diversity.

The Power of a Paradigm Shift

As I look back to the beginning of my career in business, I was extremely fortunate to have worked for an American business legend, Norman Brinker. Winner of the 1985 Horatio Alger Award and founder of Steak and Ale restaurants, Brinker is one of America's visionary entrepreneurs and one of my greatest teachers. His principles of teamwork and belief in others serve as a model for modern business leadership. Under his guidance, I was able to expand my education on the value of diversity and teamwork.

This journey began in the late 1970s when I accepted a job in the government relations department at S&A Restaurant Corp. Fresh off the farm with a degree in business education and an aspiration to be a businesswoman, my quest to climb the corporate ladder began. I'll never forget the first time I met Stephen Covey. It had to be in the early 1980s, several years before he published his inspiring national bestseller, *The Seven Habits of Highly Effective People*. Norman Brinker, a strong advocate of employee empowerment and principle-centered leadership, frequently invited Dr. Covey to Dallas to conduct workshops for his management team.

On that memorable day, Dr. Covey taught me about the power of a paradigm shift. It has continued to serve me dearly. He divided the room in half. The participants on the right side were shown a drawing that looked like a gnarled old woman, perhaps seventy or eighty years old. The participants on the left side were shown a drawing of a beautiful young woman around twenty-five years old. Each group had about 10 seconds to review the picture. Then Dr. Covey projected a third picture for the entire group to see that combined the images of both the young woman and the old woman. That's when my lesson began. When he asked some participants to describe what they saw in the third picture, I could hardly believe their responses. The people on the left side of the room described a very young beautiful woman. However, I was looking at the same picture and saw a very unattractive old woman with a large nose and protruding chin. How could that be? I tried to see the picture from another frame of reference but just couldn't see anything except the old woman. Remember, I had been conditioned for 10 seconds to see an old woman. A co-worker of mine from the left side of the room finally approached the screen and started tracing and explaining what he saw. He pointed to the young woman's necklace—it looked like the old woman's mouth to me. He traced her jaw line—it looked like the old woman's nostril to me. Finally, we got it! I saw the beautiful young woman and he saw the old woman. I found it amazing how powerfully conditioning affects our perceptions, our paradigms.

Dr. Covey taught us that "the more aware we are of our basic paradigms, maps, or assumptions and the extent to which we have been influenced by our experience, the more we can take responsibility for those paradigms, examine them, test them against reality, listen to others, and be open to their perceptions, thereby getting a larger picture and a far more objective view." I'll never forget this. If 10 seconds could have such an impact on my perspective, what must a lifetime of conditioning do? Dr. Covey said, "Valuing the differences is the essence of synergy. The person who is truly effective has the humility and reverence to recognize his own perceptual limitations and to appreciate the rich resources available through interaction with the hearts and minds of other human beings. That person values the differences because those differences add to his knowledge, to his understanding of reality. When we're left to our own experiences, we constantly suffer from shortage of data." As a reminder of this valuable lesson, I've kept copies of the pictures. To this day, when I look at the third picture I still see the old woman first. However, I'm able to quickly shift my perspective and see the face of the beautiful young woman present in the same picture.

Learn from Different Nationalities

As we study the great saints of history, we see they have personified the ideals of all lands and have embodied the highest aspirations of all religions. Paramahansa Yogananda suggests we seek from different nationalities those qualities we ought to follow or adopt in our own behavior. For example, he liked the American's "go ahead" temperament. He also liked the English tenacity; the freedom from race consciousness of the French; the exactness of the German mentality; the Chinese morality; and the Hindu spirituality. Paramahansa Yogananda said that we are meant to learn from all different nationalities, to select their best qualities and adopt them in our own behavior.

I was told many years ago that each individual is born with a special gift—a gift so unique that if each utilizes that gift, he or she can make a contribution to the world in a way no one else can. Think about that for a moment. Every individual, including you, possesses some special talent, some unique capability, with which a significant contribution to the world civilization can be made. Wow! If we all start living our potential, just imagine how fast we would evolve.

We can produce synergy by engaging in a constructive exchange among individuals and nations of their best features.

We should discern and emulate the virtues and ignore the faults. Paramahansa Yogananda said, "On earth God is trying to evolve the universal art of right living by encouraging in men's hearts feelings of brotherhood and appreciation for others. He has therefore permitted no nation to be complete in itself. To the members of each race He has given some special aptitude, some unique genius, with which they may make a distinctive contribution to the world civilization."

Prayer for World Unity

Let us pray in our hearts for a League of Souls and a United World. Though we may seem divided by race, creed, color, class, and political prejudices, still, as children of the one God we are able in our souls to feel brotherhood and world unity. May we work for the creation of a United World in which every nation will be a useful part, guided by God through man's enlightened conscience.

In our hearts we can all learn to be free from hate and selfishness. Let us pray for harmony among the nations, that they march hand in hand through the gate of a fair new civilization.

—*Metaphysical Meditations*

Working Together: Building a Sense of Community

For the last four years I have worked with some incredible individuals in the promotional products industry. This group has presented me with some challenges, encouraged me to be creative and innovative, and blessed me by expanding my heart. Most recently, the majority of my time has been dedicated to creating a sense of community among the national association (PPA) and the twenty-nine regional associations across the country.

In the industry's recent past, PPA and the regional associations have operated separately and independently of one another, restricting vast resources, stifling creativity and innovative energies. Now, a new energy has emerged through the Regional Association Advisory Council, and the momentum is building for this group to become the visionary leader that will help guide the industry into a successful and profitable future through partnerships.

These new and exciting partnerships actually began last year when colleagues came together for the first time in a spirit of mutual respect and authenticity. This group gathered to explore ways to work together for the benefit of the promotional products industry as a whole. One of the goals was to create a healthy environment where a diversity of views and opinions could be respectfully exchanged and considered. Participants came to the meeting prepared to be open and honest, recognizing that there would be differences of opinions and that only through honoring this diversity could the differences be resolved. The challenge was to utilize these differences to create new, exciting partnerships—partnerships geared to service and contribution. The essence of synergy is to value differences—to respect them, to build on their strengths, and to compensate for their weaknesses.

The nurturing and diversity we seek is a balance between the good of each individual association and the good of the industry—a balance between short-term and long-term focus. It is a nurturing that considers the impact of action upon the industry for the next century. We must create a way to structure our collective efforts so that everyone prospers. No one group should prosper at the expense of another. One only needs to look at the history of the American Indians to witness their compassion and love for those generations yet unborn. Their leaders are men of vision, instructed to make every decision on behalf of the seventh generation to come.

If we are committed, communicative, and creative enough, we can foster conditions that nurture the potentials of both individual and collective excellence by building quality working relationships. As the rate of change continues to escalate, it is clear that ways of working based solely on competition and individualism must give way to wiser ways of working more cooperatively and supportively in teams.

This new kind of community building is a process. I encourage each of us to honor our diversity and work together. We have the power to decide where to focus our strength. We can either continue to empower a defunct structure or shift into a new awareness, with purpose and open minds and hearts, and begin to lay the foundation to build unity through cooperative partnerships.

The associations are just ingredients in the promotional products industry. The members are also ingredients in the larger commerce world we are part of. At the same time, we are part of the governments, religions, and social service agencies that bind us together, as the liquids bind the flour in bread dough. Conflicts are uncomfortable, and as for the bread baking in the oven, temperature needs to be controlled. But once we come together, once we become part of a family, a company, an association, a community, or a culture, we can never return to what we were before.

As Chief Seattle said in the 1850s, "This we know—All things are connected like the blood that unites us. Whatever we do to the web, we do to ourselves." Twentieth-century physicist David Bohm agrees: "This notion that all these fragments are separately existent is evidently an illusion, and this illusion cannot do other than lead to endless conflict and confusion." Scientists across the world are more readily accepting the views that the universe is an interconnected conscious whole. Tennyson says in his poem *Ulysses*, "I am part of all that I have met." We are the generation with the responsibility and option to choose the path of partnership. If the American Indian culture offers us a metaphor, perhaps we will come to understand that it's important we have vision and make decisions with future generations in mind. Let us celebrate the magnificence of our diversity and evolve beyond where we presently are. This will require courage, boldness, and deep commitment.

Coming Together

I learned these lessons on the farm, I learned these lessons in my mother's kitchen, and over time, I learned these lessons in the business world. For social change to occur, for our communities to become safer, for our businesses to become healthier, all the ingredients must come together. We must realize that it is the coming together and merging of our interests that is important. In order to produce synergy, we must recognize and accept that we must work together, that tension and conflict are part of the process, that we must honor our diversity and understand that too much "heat" can destroy the harmony everyone is seeking to achieve.

Michael G. Welp, Ph.D., leads EqualVoice, a consulting firm that helps organizations build lasting collaborative environments by providing tools for conflict, learning, and change. He focuses on diversity as a source of transformation and unification. Welp's successful approach to conflict resolution runs counter to prevailing wisdom, focusing on generating more voices of difference between people, not less. Recent clients include Shell Oil, Pillsbury, ConAgra, and US Army Corp of Engineers.

Welp co-founded www.WhiteMenAndDiversity.com, a partnership working with organizations to engage white men as full diversity partners. His background includes a year of facilitating interracial teambuilding for South African corporations. A popular keynote speaker, he also co-leads the White Men's Caucus on Eliminating Racism, Sexism and Homophobia in Organizations. His dissertation, *Pathways to Diversity for White Males*, can be downloaded from www.equalvoice.com.

9

The Treasures and Challenges of Diversity for White Males

Michael G. Welp

The room is still as people around the circle lean forward to listen. Quiet moans and twitches of discomfort float about as a woman recounts her story. Among her flowing tears and deep pain are the fragments of an experience from childhood when she was denied use of a public drinking fountain. The fountain was off limits, marked "For Whites Only." Inside, my heart grew heavy. I felt paralyzed as I heard this story of oppression. I knew of our country's segregated history, but it never felt as real as it became that moment. Why had it not been real before? I don't remember the details of her story. What I carry is the depth of pain this colleague held. It is one of a few key experiences in my life that catalyzed my transformative journey toward advocating inclusion and equity.

In my colleague's story the oppression was overt, the fountain clearly marked with a printed sign. Harder to grasp are the more subtle ways in which discrimination continues, fed by passivity, fear, and avoidance. As often as I have successfully confronted discrimination or participated in open dialogues around diversity issues, I can also recall feeling too hesitant to confront or too scared to talk openly about touchy issues. Diversity challenges me, like many things in life. It brings forth my strongest and weakest parts. Embracing diversity thus means dancing with my own shadow. I am glad because this is one of the more significant dances in my ongoing process of growth.

Some of the most important lessons I've learned during the past decade have centered on the touchy topic of white males and diversity. The media has focused on the worry, anger, and resentment of white males. However, while I have found my journey, at times, painful, I have also found the pathway toward diversity to contain priceless treasures.

Writing about white males is tricky for several reasons. We often resist seeing ourselves as a group. We see women, people of color, and others as groups, but we tend to see ourselves only as individuals. We need to transcend the "either/or" question. We are *both* individuals *and* members of the white male group. We must look at both realities to comprehend and respond to issues around diversity. Others see us as a group, so we must too in order to understand their reality. A second challenge is that acknowledging our membership in the white male group can seem to imply denying other differences such as class, religion, age, sexual orientation, and ethnicity within the white male group. But again, transcending the "either/or" question, we are a white male group *and* there are differences that split white males. To understand issues of diversity, we must move from either/or to both/and logic. I am *both* white male *and* American born, heterosexual, in my mid-30s, raised Catholic, upper middle class, ablebodied, mixed northern-European heritage, and introverted. My writing about white males is oriented toward my membership in these categories as well. White males with other backgrounds will have different experiences. Acknowledging the white male group, collectively and with individual differences, is one part of the whole puzzle and is a critical piece often overlooked.

Diversity Is Only Half the Picture

As a high school senior, I spent a summer with a family in northern Germany. What struck me most was how similar we were to each other. The similarities put the differences into perspective. Difference and sameness are a polarity with each being defined in part by the other. Barry Johnson illuminates polarity dynamics in *Polarity Management*. He explains the paradox that in order to gain the benefits of one pole, you must also pursue the benefits of the other. To stimulate reflection, I often ask people: If you were stranded on a desert island, would you rather be with twelve people exactly like you or twelve people who are totally different? Most people recognize they'd want people with totally different skills and resources. But in reality you would want *both* similarities *and* differences. Things like a common language would be helpful. In this hypothetical situation you would have something else in common, a goal to survive. To understand diversity, you have to involve something at the other end of the pole, like unity or community. My explorations of diversity throughout the world have always been informed by the commonality of the human family. Seeing a smile or hearing a deep chuckle from a co-worker in South Africa served to bridge the gaps of language, race, generation, and many other differences. Wisdom comes from seeking insights into both similarities and differences and recognizing that both are always present in some way. To do this I must know myself, my culture, and my motives since it is easy to erroneously project similarity onto those things I like and difference onto those things I don't like.

Learning Our White Male Culture

Knowing our own culture, and thus knowing ourselves, can often be hardest for white males. The benefit of being the dominant culture is that others must either conform to it or know it well enough to work around it. In writing about white males, I speak especially about heterosexual white males, since ours is the most dominant culture. The cost of this privilege is that as straight white males, we often have the least awareness of our own culture. Leadership consultant and author Robert Terry summed up this dynamic when he said, "To be white is not to have to think about it." Terry also wrote a Parable of Ups and Downs about the dynamics of privilege and calls this dynamic "dumb-upness." Obviously the costs of this privilege are ignorance and lack of awareness, which often translate into lack of choice and a reactive stance. Being a part of the dominant culture can thus become a prison of limited awareness. Exploring diversity is the key to this prison: It raises awareness and opens the door to choices previously unknown and unreachable, for each culture holds many gifts of wisdom concerning how to live in this world.

Thus, I have found that I need to leave my culture in order to understand it. Just as a fish is the last to understand the concept of water, it is by exploring another reality that we come to more clearly see our own reality. The paradox is that in order to understand who we are, we must understand who we are not. As a guest on the Rosebud Indian Reservation in South Dakota a few years ago, I heard a week of storytelling and saw what it means for a culture to have a strong oral tradition. Through this, I realized my culture does not rely on oral stories as a mode of passing on the culture. I can't change unless I first realize I have choices. My journeys to other cultures have shown me the choices my culture has made and have expanded what I perceive as the choices before me.

Many white males don't believe we have a distinct culture. Culture is something others have. I didn't understand the dominant straight white male American culture in which I was raised until I began to look at other cultures both within and outside the United States. I came to understand my culture as having a strong focus on action, as opposed to being, reflection, and stability. In my culture *time* has a linear aspect, focuses on the future, and controls many social interactions, including for example how long my church service lasts. This is not true in many other cultures where the length of meetings, such as church services, depends on the energy felt in the moment. Edwin Nichols, a diversity consultant, notes how cultures traced back to European history learned a concept of time as linear due to short crop growing seasons. Being task oriented and allowing time to control activities was a matter of survival. Cultures where plants grew all year long came to think of time as more cyclical. It is important to gain an insider's view of the culture rather than interpret it from an outsider's perspective. Someone from a linear concept of time is likely to misinterpret the behavior of someone from a cyclical concept of time if they haven't gained an inside view of the culture.

Similarly, I have heard white Americans talk about Jesse Jackson as being too emotional and almost out of control. As Thomas Kochman describes in his book *Black and White Styles in Conflict*, for black American culture, the presence of emotion signifies truth. But in the white male American culture, it can be the opposite. Truth is attached more to the concept of being rational and in control. It is easy to misjudge another culture from one's own cultural perspective. Here I am reminded, as Angeles Arrien mentions in her book *The Four-Fold Way*, that the Latin term for the word *respect* means "the willingness to look again."

My white male culture values the importance of the individual over the importance of the collective. In the United States the saying is, "The squeaky wheel gets the grease," while in Japan it's, "The nail that sticks up gets hammered down." For the white male American culture, self-reliance and independence are valued over harmony and interdependence. We commonly "borrow" a quarter promising to return it, while in some other countries to settle out debts is to threaten to end the relationship. One aspect of my culture that I treasure is the espoused value of equality, though we have a ways to go in achieving it. Some other cultures in the world do not value or espouse equality. Related to that is our looser and more flexible concept of hierarchy than some other cultures in the world. The themes of the dominant white American culture have been well documented by Edward Hall, Geert Hofstede, Nancy Adler, Gary Weaver, and many others in the field of intercultural research. It is very important to note that many of these studies focused on white males and thus describe the dominant white male American culture. Examining gender differences illuminated by writers such as Debra Tannen, Riane Eisler, and Carol Gilligan is very important. These authors discuss the different values placed on relationships, hierarchy, and other cultural variables. It is vital to remember that cultural patterns describe group tendencies, and individuals vary within each culture. Understanding cultural tendencies helps us to understand our predispositions. Through reading and experiencing other cultures, we begin to truly understand our culture and ourselves.

Putting ourselves in the position of being a minority can generate learning by thrusting ourselves out of the "dumb-up" role. In doing so, we can become preoccupied with issues of inclusion and noticing what gets us included or excluded. This is an experience many people who are not straight white males struggle with everyday. I have experienced concern about inclusion when I was the only white person in cross-cultural travels and community gatherings; the only heterosexual attending a gay, lesbian, bisexual, and transgender church community; or the only man in all-women groups. I have also experienced being on the edge of groups through shyness. These experiences sensitize me to the dynamics of inclusion and the energy drain required to deal with situations that are not inclusive.

I have found many benefits in truly understanding myself and my cultural values. Only when I am aware of my culture can I truly appreciate it. Also only when I am aware of my culture can I begin to avoid imposing it on others. I stop seeing it as universal reality and begin to see it as one culture among many. I have learned from social psychologist Edgar Schein to view cultures as "shared solutions to universal problems of external adaption and internal integration." These solutions gradually become accepted as assumptions that are taken for granted. Sometimes my culture's "solutions" have dysfunctional side-effects around which I would like to develop choices. For instance, my culture has a strong belief that we can control our circumstances and shape our destinies. As a result, when we fail, we have no way to explain the failure except to blame ourselves. I believe this is why three-quarters of all suicides in this country are committed by white males. Edwin Nichols, former researcher at the National Institute for Mental Health, has studied this dynamic. He noted that during the closing of steel mills in the 1970s, for every tenth of one percent rise in unemployment, five hundred white males committed suicide. This may have also been the result of a loss of identity for these men, since in our culture most of our identity typically comes from what we do. Most other cultures do not define identity so exclusively by occupation. Still others emphasize harmony with the world instead of control. By recognizing my culture as *one* solution to universal problems instead of viewing it as *the* solution, can I begin to transcend the dysfunctional aspects of my culture. I recognize other possible choices. Exploring diversity then becomes the key to unbinding cultural chains.

Challenges on the Diversity Path

My pathway toward advocating inclusion and equity has felt steep, and at times the load has been heavy. Heaviest is the pain I feel when I recognize my unconscious contributions to oppression. It is the pain of ignorance, of swallowing unchallenged cultural assumptions and realizing I am living on shaky untested ground. Being open to the possibility that I have caused additional unrecognized hurt and pain leaves me feeling exposed and raw, putting me in touch with my own incompetence and humility. This is a very emotional place to be for a white male whose culture typically values rational over emotional intelligence. As diversity consultant Tom Kochman explains, "Nobody wants to be caught with egg on our face." Kochman also notes that culturally, white males believe they "have to have it all right," which comes from the premise that "it's wrong to be wrong." This makes the incompetence and humility I feel even more intense. White males culturally do not tolerate uncertainty well, often responding with reactive postures. But to travel the pathway to diversity is to go to a place of not knowing. Just when we think we've got the world figured out and know what the rules are, we find out there are many more sets of rules. Humility knocks at our door and says there is more to learn. Often fear answers the door and says, "I'm afraid about what I'm going to learn about myself." It can be hard at this point to remember that our gift in this process is a greater clarity of who we are and a reclaiming of choices around who we would like to become.

On my path I have also felt both guilt and shame. Sometimes I have found them to motivate my learning process. Other times they can slow my movement and wipe away my momentum. Chere Brown, founder of the National Coalition Building Institute, notes that "guilt is the glue that holds prejudice together." Guilt can serve to catalyze or immobilize the learning process. Author Shelby Steele notes that guilt can be dangerous, for it tends to draw us into self-preoccupation. Thus, guilt can be a motivator only if it is contained, so that one can focus *beyond* striving for innocence. I have sometimes found my motivation limited to proving that I'm a "good guy," especially since, as a white male, I can get caught in the belief that I "have to have it all right." Guilt helps us understand the weight of these issues, but it is important to travel onward to the field beyond ideas of right-doing and wrong-doing. Inequality has its own momentum. If we are inactive and neutral, striving only for innocence but not for change, we continue to allow that momentum to build.

As I actively engage in this struggle, being in a place of not knowing connects me to my humility and humanness. When I share this openly, I find I am open to receiving the compassion and forgiveness of others. I only have a piece of the puzzle, a part of the whole truth, and I rely on others to build a greater whole with me. To do this involves taking risks and moving toward my fear. Through these struggles on the path to diversity, I have found a spiritual connection to the whole. It is a movement from thinking about different cultures as "right or wrong" to "right or left." As the poet Rumi said: "Out beyond ideas of right-doing and wrong-doing there is a field. I'll meet you there." It is important not to solely rely on people of color, women, and others to educate us white males about diversity. White males also can help each other. When we help ourselves and each other, we will find others willing to help us too.

A few years ago I lived for a year in Lesotho and South Africa where I led week-long Outward Bound courses focused on inter-racial team building for mining companies and other South African corporations. Working there, I found people of different colors had been kept separate from each other and socialized to fear each other. I believe there is a very similar dynamic for many people in the United States. In South Africa, people had never formed the types of relationships across racial lines that would enable them to test and challenge assumptions they were taught to believe about each other. One white miner had been told by his wife that she would divorce him if he slept in the same room as the black miners. On a youth course, a white girl had been told by her parents that if she ate out of the same pot as black kids, she would get sick. Through the structure of an Outward Bound course, which requires interdependent teamwork, people of both cultures found they shared many of the same strengths and fears. That helped them to balance the polarity of difference and commonal-ity, which is a major source of creative tension in forming community. Weaving together a community means moving through fear to discover real differences *and* real commonality.

This was the same experience I had when I heard the story of my friend's experience at the water fountain. I asked myself why I had never truly felt the pain and impact of segregation before hearing her story. I had not yet built the depth of relation-ship across racial lines necessary to truly share and hear another's reality, learn about real differences, and discover commonality.

One does not need to travel to South Africa to learn about diversity. Diversity is everywhere. Pay attention to differences you have that create for you conditions of inclusion or exclusion. Notice similar dynamics for others. How do the places you work and live tolerate the presence of different cultural realities? Are there parts of yourself that you have to leave outside the door? Besides cultural differences, look at individual style, expression, and skills. Instruments like the Myers-Briggs Type Indicator help us see strengths others bring that complement ours. As we discovered in thinking about who we'd like to be stranded with on a desert island, we come to value each other's unique abilities and resources.

Traveling the diversity pathway promises to expand the learning skills of white males because it demands that we cope with powerful emotions, tolerate ambiguity, and deepen our reflections. The realities of diversity make the world more complex. Thomas Kochman points out that the Golden Rule—do unto others as you would like them to do unto you—assumes that others want the same that you want. This is not true in a world of diversity; people want and value different things. Thus, skills in tolerating and managing this complexity are demanded. Responding to the presence of diversity strengthens the learning skills so needed in today's world.

Treasures on the Diversity Path

There is a strong business case for diversity. Organizations that understand and value diversity gain better access to diverse markets, locally and overseas, and they benefit from better access to the diversity of human resources they have available. They enjoy better relations with local communities and government and avoid costly litigation. They achieve what diversity consultant Chuck Shelton calls a "sustainable collaborative advantage." Learning the skills involved in honoring and working with diversity helps us become the kind of flexible and responsive people needed in today's world.

In addition, I have found other, more personal treasures as well. First is a greater clarity and appreciation for who I am and a reclaiming of choice about who I would like to become. I am not the same person I was when I began my diversity path. I am more myself, which includes more of some aspects of the white male culture and less of others. I have removed some of the blind spots of my privilege, which has given me humility, compassion, and freedom from "dumb-upness." I have a greater connection with myself, my emotions, and my strengths and weaknesses. My need to conform is lessened as I recognize the diversity within me. I have also become more bicultural, able to function in different cultural norms according to the needs of those around me, as well as my own. I understand more how others perceive both myself and the groups of which I am a member. I am caught less frequently in the traps of either/or logic and am better able to think beyond right and wrong. My abilities to tolerate ambiguity, to reflect, and to learn have increased. This process has led me to a greater sense of connection with others both near me and around the world. I see myself as part of a larger whole. Here lies the heart of the journey: Exploring my white male identity allows me to become more of who I am and connects me to a world much greater than myself.

Norman Lear has had a distinguished career as a producer, director, comedy writer, screenwriter, political and social activist, and philanthropist. Known to the American public as the creator of Archie Bunker and *All in the Family*, Lear's entertainment career includes numerous TV and motion picture credits. He has the distinction of being one of the first seven people inducted into the Television Academy Hall of Fame (1984).

Lear is a noted activist on behalf of human rights and civil liberties. He is the founder of People For the American Way (1980), The Business Enterprise Trust (1989), and co-founder of the American Civil Liberties Foundation of Southern California. He is also the co-owner of an original copy of the Declaration of Independence, which is traveling in an unprecedented nationwide tour between 2001 and 2004, involving communities across the country.

He is currently Chairman of ACT III Communications, a multimedia holding company.

10

Unity without Uniformity

Norman Lear

A few years ago, I was pleased and honored—and amused—to address the National Press Club on the subject of faith, vision, and values in American life. Pleased because I have so many friends in the working press, I looked forward to seeing them again and felt honored because of the enormous respect I have for the institution of a free press in a free society. The amusement was occasioned by a vivid memory from a Sunday afternoon more than a decade earlier.

Whenever I am feeling good about myself—as I felt on the day that I prepared to appear before that illustrious group—I'm reminded of my late Jewish mother, who had a knack for doing whatever she could to deflate that feeling. I had phoned her in Bridgeport, Connecticut, to tell her that the Academy of Television Arts and Sciences had selected her son as one of its first inductees. I said, "Mom, the TV academy has just established a Hall of Fame and guess who the first inductees will be? Milton Berle, William Paley, David Sarnoff, Lucille Ball, Edward R. Murrow, Paddy Chayevsky, and me." After a short beat, my mother said: "Look, if that's what they want to do, who am I to say?"

She's been gone for eight years now, but if my mother knew what I am up to these days—devoting time to speaking and writing about the spiritual state of America her response, no doubt, would be similar. I am, after all, that Hollywood guy responsible for Archie Bunker, George Jefferson, Mary Hartman and Maude Finley—some of the least introspective and spiritually inclined characters ever to appear on television. What could I possibly have to say about the mysterious realm known as the human soul?

My window on the world—and my window into the American quest for meaning and values—has been the some forty-five years I've spent In television and film where, in trying to connect with millions of viewers, I have developed a rather keen appreciation of the troubles and joys of ordinary families, struggling to do the best they can in our crazy times. Observing our national quirks and quiddities and dramatizing Americans as they try to cope with their times have taught me a great deal about our people and institutions, and about the national psyche.

I am also a human being and, like every other human being, I was born with the capacity—I call it the Original Gift—to ponder these matters, to seek understanding and transcendence. An ancient piece of Jewish wisdom stated that a man should have a garment with two pockets. In the first should be a piece of paper on which is written, "I am but dust and ashes." But in the second pocket, that ancient wisdom advised, there should be a piece of paper on which is written: "For me the world was created." I have never run across a bit of philosophy that has resonated with me more.

I can't imagine how difficult it must be today for American families to believe that the world was created for them, so awash in anguish are they as they deal with that world. There is no longer any dispute that the foundations of modern society, especially here in America, are being shaken to their depths. We are living through a wrenching transition—economically, culturally, spiritually. The old certainties are gone, and the new ones have yet to crystalize.

We need only think back a generation or two to see how much has changed. The institutions of the church, the family, education and civil authority—the world that Walter Lippman referred to as "that old ancestral order," once serving as gyroscopes of stability for our lives—no longer command the same authority or respect. Once responsible for purveying values from one generation to another, and for giving a deep sense of order, continuity, and higher meaning to our culture, now these institutions are beleaguered and divided.

As the influence of the old ancestral order has waned, it has become increasingly apparent that American business has come to fill the vacuum. More than any other institution, business has become the fountainhead of values in our society. Joseph Campbell had an arresting metaphor to describe the shift. In medieval times, he said, as one approached a city, the tallest strut on the skyline was the church and its steeple. Subsequently, as the power and influence of the church gave way to kings and rulers, the castle dominated the skyline. Today, as one approaches the city, the most commanding structures are the skyscrapers, the cathedrals of modern business.

To Campbell's marvelous metaphor I would add the satellite uplinks and spires that now adorn our business cathedrals, trumpeting the phenomenon of television, itself a great American industry, piping the messages of American business into every American home, by the dozen per half hour, on sets that research tells us may be on as much as seven hours per day.

What is notable about this fountainhead of values in American life is not simply the message that "We are what we consume," although that is hardly insignificant. It is, rather, the overweening commitment of American business, not to qualitative values, but to quantitative values—to numbers. There are no villains here. Nobody "ordered" it; it just happened. But this steadily growing obsession with numbers has transformed our culture—and our sense of ourselves as well.

It is no exaggeration to say that we live in a world utterly dominated by numbers. We define ourselves, our values and our aspirations by SAT scores, Nielsen ratings, box office grosses, cost/benefit analyses, quarterly reports, bottom lines, and polls, polls, polls—all of which exert an iron grip on our sense of the possible and on our very identities. We have become a numbers-oriented culture that places its faith in what we can graph, chart, or count, and is suspicious of the unquantifiable, the intuitive, the mysterious.

A culture that becomes a stranger to its inner human needs is a culture that has lost touch with the best of its humanity—that fertile but neglected realm that is the wellspring for human creativity and morality; that portion of ourselves that impels us to create art and literature, and study ethics, philosophy, and history—the part of our being that gives rise to our sense of awe and wonder, and our longing for a higher order of meaning.

As a student of the American psyche, at no time in my life

can I remember our culture being so estranged from this essential part of itself. One can see it in the loss of faith in leaders and institutions, the cynicism, selfishness, and erosion of civility, and the hunger for connectedness that stalks our nation today.

Between Lewis Mumford, the great historian, studying the fall of Rome, and Alexis de Tocqueville, studying the American character more than a century and a half ago, I think we find, perfectly described, where America is today. Mumford concluded that "Rome fell not because of political invasions, It collapsed through a 'barbarization from within.'"

And de Tocqueville, studying us when our republic was still young, wrote: "I confess I believe our democratic society to have much less to fear from boldness than from paltriness of aim. What frightens me most is the danger that, amid all the constant trivial preoccupations of private life, ambition may lose both its force and its greatness that human passions may grow gentler and at the same time baser, with the result that the progress of the body social may become daily quieter and less aspiring."

De Tocqueville's prediction has come true, The contemporary American condition is quieter and less aspiring. The human passions have grown gentler and at the same time baser. Our culture is preoccupied with all matter of trivia and harbors few ambitions to greatness. And, as in Mumford's description of Rome, our culture is indeed suffering from a leeching away of meaning, a "barbarization from within."

To scan the cultural landscape today is to see the symptoms of this condition—the burgeoning "army of the irrelevant"—the under-class, the homeless, the unemployed, the survivalists and militia, all the angry middle-class Americans so alienated from their own government and culture, Look also at the growth of racism and hate crimes, the mindless massacres, the children killing children, deteriorating cities, and a crumbling infrastructure.

What does it say about a culture when nearly one-third of all babies are born to single, unwed mothers? Among black women the figure is 62 percent, and in some areas, 80 percent. Add to this the mess that is healthcare, not to mention the environment— that slow-motion apocalypse of acid rain, ozone depletion, and global warming.

How did we get here? And what can we do about it? The answers, I believe, point well beyond the conventional categories of public discourse-politics, the marketplace, journalism. We need to reposition the discussion into a larger context, in the realm of the human soul. What kind of cultural "home" have we created for the soul in our politics and commerce, entertainment and journalism? How can we begin to acquire a firm spiritual and moral footing in the midst of an avalanche of change reaching into every corner of our society?

As a writer, I always ask myself how those people euphemistically called the "little guys" experience all of this—those millions of Americans who are becoming economically expendable. Every now and then I try to imagine what's going on in the heart and mind of an average American worker—I call him Bill.

Bill and his wife Louise are doing their best to live on two incomes that don't total even $49,000 per year, which, according to the statistics, puts them near the top of the bottom three-fifths. Three kids, one in college hoping like hell she can afford to stay there, and another one getting out of high school in June. This one says he doesn't want college, but Bill wonders if maybe he's just saying that because he knows his parents are having trouble figuring out how they're going to send him.

Bill grew up in a terrific area called a neighborhood (remember that word?), with lots of friends and family, all of them living up the street and down the street and across the street from one another. Now he and his family live in a tract where the word "neighborhood" is seldom heard. It's 40 minutes of carpooling to work for Bill every day and maybe an hour and ten minutes getting home at night. "Work used to be only ten minutes away, until they shut down the plant," Bill says. "My father and his father and all his brothers worked at the plant, generation after generation, except for some of us kids who escaped to become druggists, or dentists, or accountants, which our parents, of course, were always pushing us to do! But no matter what—there was always the plant, like a floor under our lives. Who knew the floor had a trap door?"

Something's wrong, and Bill knows it. He sees standup comics, all dressed up like a million bucks, or dressed down in jeans with rips that are supposed to make them seem like "ordinary" people—all of them laughing and having a good old time. "Nobody I know is having a good time," Bill says. Most of them are struggling to get it right, rolling over after Letterman and Leno go off the air, feeling a little guilty, maybe even a little ashamed, because "it just isn't adding up for us like it is for all them on the late shows, and like it is for the people in the TV ads whooping and hollering and hoisting their beers, as if they didn't have a care in the world."

Inside, sometimes, Bill feels like an empty room. He finds himself wondering more and more about church. "Maybe its because we stopped going," Bill says. "We went when the kids were little—but later, when so much else was going on in their lives, and what was going on in church didn't much grab 'em, we didn't press. He says he doesn't much miss church, because he and Louise weren't getting much out of it, either, "yet we do talk about it all the time. We talk about what was missing around our dinner table through the years. We talk about what's missing now."

Bill likes to tell me about his best friend's wife, Lil, who's gotten into all kinds of unusual things—like a book called *The Tibetan Book of the Living and Dying.* And then Lil's next door neighbor has a set of "healing from within" tapes that she uses for meditation. Bill says he doesn't know what to make of meditation. "Sounds weird to me—sitting around on the floor with their legs under them, listening to some voice that puts them in the mood so they can just—well, sit—emptying their minds is what they tell us. I couldn't empty my mind with a putty knife!" He says he remembers a time when their friends couldn't wait for the next paperback from Jackie Collins or Judith Krantz. Now he's into something called Zen. "Vince Kuznick and Zen—I think I'm in the Twilight Zone!"

A lot of people Bill knows—and more he reads about—are into some of those twelve-step, self-help programs because they're overweight or want to stop drinking or wanting sex all the time "They're all the time talking about 'letting go' and giving themselves to a Higher Power—making the kind of stained-glass talk that sounds like it ought to be coming out of churches." Finally, Bill and Louise decided to start dipping into some of that stuff themselves. They got the Joseph Campbell tapes and the John Bradshaw lectures—and to their surprise, they got something out of them. "Even where I work they've got these guys coming in and talking to us about 'circles of compassion' and 'community' and 'spirit in the workplace' and all like that," Bill says.

The main questions Bill finds himself asking are these: Isn't all this stuff stirring up the same feelings the church is supposed to be stirring up? What happened? Why isn't the church speaking to us anymore? And how far from the church can some of this stuff get? Like, at the supermarket, I see this throwaway newspaper full of stories about crystal worshippers, and deep breathers, and dream therapy groupies, and other California lala." Bill says he's doing his best to figure out the environmentalist tree-worshippers who see God In the ecology. And the women's magazines with those pictures of models walking down the runway in monks' robes wearing crucifixes.

"It must add up to something but what?" Bill asks. "I keep asking that question they made the movie about: 'What's it all about, Alfie?' You want to give me and my family something for Christmas? Help me with that question."

I don't know if this will help, Bill, but you're not seeing anything different from the rest of the world. In a dangerous, volatile world, so different from what it was a scant 50 years ago; a world now governed by numbers that seek to rationalize every corner of human existence; a world in which it seems increasingly difficult to experience a sense of community and the fellowship of other human beings; a technological, scientific world in which to most the presence of God seems highly problematic, it should not be surprising that people like you, Bill—and you are everywhere—seek desperately for spiritual connection.

And yet, Bill says the church doesn't speak to him anymore. I suspect that's because the church has stopped listening. The entire culture seems oblivious to this aspect of his pain. Why is it that most political leaders fail to see the connection between Bill's deep disappointment, disaffection, and unhappiness, and the spiritual hunger that gnaws at him? And why do so many church leaders continue to believe blindly that spiritual connection is simply a matter of accepting the right religious doctrine or the most venerated sacred text? They don't seem to understand that many in their own congregations, regular churchgoers, also relate to Bill's searching. They confuse religious piety with spiritual connection.

It's a point I once tried to make in an odd article in *The Washington Post*. The spiritual life of the human species, I wrote, occupies a much larger, more heterogeneous realm than any organized religion can lay claim to. A noted conservative columnist concluded a week later that my spirituality was pathetically deficient. Don't you know, he essentially said, nobody needs anything more than the Ten Commandments and the Bible. "Spare us the group hug rediscovery of the inner-self-cum-true meaning of life," he snorted, giving a brisk, patriotic salute to that Old Time Religion.

Now, excuse me for believing that religious experience ought to bear a closer resemblance to Love Thy Neighbor, to the essence of the Sermon on the Mount—to a group hug, if you will—than to pietistic pistol-whipping.

We see a similar self-righteous intolerance displayed toward fellow humans who happen to be living unsanctioned, alternative spiritual lives—to those respectable, middle-class Americans my imaginary friend Bill referred to, who buy all those bestselling books about God, angels, the spirit, the soul and death, which often constitute half of the top 15 paperback bestsellers. Where are their cathedrals and bishops? the traditionalists demand. Where are their theologies and sacred traditions? Why don't they worship the same way we do?

Let me speak personally for a moment. I consider myself deeply religious. I am a Jew and I love my people and our culture. I could not be prouder of what, in our long history, we have brought to the world. But that is not what makes me religious, What makes me religious is the way I experience all of creation; what makes me religious is the way I experience the Almighty, and, perhaps, the way I experience life and the way I try to live it.

There was a book called *Edith the Good* written about Edith Bunker of "All in the Family." The author's thesis was that Edith's every reflexive reaction to any situation was what the writer thought Jesus' reaction might be. He was right; that's how Edith was conceived. Now, I'm not in Edith's league by any means— though I ache to be—because everything in me tells me the world would he an exquisite place to live, were everyone able to respond to life as Jesus did.

I am reconciled to the fact that not everyone who reads these words will agree that I qualify as a religious person, because I have not expressed myself in a manner they could accept. My words, and Bill's as well, lack scripture, theology, ecclesiastical authority. Still, ever since my early twenties when I smoked my first good cigar, I have felt and said that if there was no other reason to believe in God, it would have to be Havana leaf. I have said the same thing while biting into a ripe peach, a just-ready piece of Crenshaw melon, or a great ear of sweet summer corn.

I have sensed God's presence sitting in the back of a dark theater when a comedy was playing, watching an audience of 600 strangers coming forward, rising in their seats and then falling back, as people do when they are laughing from the belly. I have fallen in love with a total stranger several aisles and many rows away at the sound of his or her distinct laugh. I have experienced God's presence in the faces of my wife, my children, my grandson—and every time throughout my working life when I have gone to bed with a second-act problem and awakened in the morning with the solution.

There was a time when I wouldn't have dared to write an essay like this. I couldn't because I didn't have the vocabulary. The language of religious expression seemed always to belong to the professionals—and I simply do not make the sounds that are heard in churches and synagogues and on television when these matters are being discussed by the pros. Then my wife, and a good friend, a noted church historian, suggested I read William James' *The Varieties of Religious Experience*. And there I was—between the lines, between the experiences.

So, now, I ask myself: Why can't I share my sense of all this—in any way I am able to express it—without being made to feel like a second-class "groper after meaning"? Because that's what I am—a groper, searching every step of the way for a better understanding. And because I am not specifically attached to any synagogue, I suppose you can call me an "unaffiliated groper."

It's a disposition that I think I've learned from my children. kids are naturally inquisitive, without guile or prejudice, and brave enough to ask any question. They are unaffiliated gropers of the first order and we all nurture that in our children. Well, at age 74, just a split-second older than my two year-old daughters and eight year-old son—at least from the perspective of the universe, God's timeline—I, too, would like to be nurtured in my sense of awe and wonder and curiosity and thirst for primary experience.

That's where I think so many of us are—that's where Bill may well be. And if we want to see Bill back in church, we had better take him as he is. Don't let him be shamed or coerced out of the conversation by the well-honed oratory of those profession-als who claim—some only by implication—that their expression of religious insight, and their expression of whatever ritual and tradition, gives them a greater right to be heard.

It is when we divide and retreat into our many religious tribes—and honor one exclusive system of religiosity over all else—that our problems really begin. "As one reads history," wrote Oscar Wilde, "one is absolutely sickened, not by the crimes that the wicked have committed, but by the punishments that the good have inflicted." I find nothing sadder than the use of religion to vilify and hurt people, all in the name of a greater good, of course. AIDS is God's retribution on immoral gays, for example; doctors who perform abortions deserve to be killed; authors and artists who say disturbing things are agents of Satan; ethnic cleansing is needed for the religiously unworthy.

I take hope in the fact that I continue to encounter other unaffiliated gropers from myriad walks of life—perhaps there are far more of us than we suppose. This corps of seekers is a far more potent source of social reconstruction than many traditionalists may imagine. Journalist Jeff Greenfield once said that if reporters had been aware of what was going on in the basements of black churches in the 1950s, they would have known that a significant social and political force was about to explode. They would have been better prepared for the emergence of people like Rosa Parks, Martin Luther King Jr., Fanny Lou Hamer and other civil rights activists.

A story of equal significance, I suspect, is building now: a buzzing, disconnected eruption of spiritual reaction to our times, operating without the sanction of the popular culture or organized religion. And it is available to any groper. But you must not be psyched out by the "experts." The time has come to begin breaking down the walls erected by both secularists and religionists, walls that prevent us from talking about this. It's too big a story. It's a story well beyond conventional religious categories.

But how can we begin to get beyond these categories and see what unites us as humans? If one were to look at a very long river, one might see flora and fauna, trees and shrubs of varying nature along the many miles of its banks. If we think of our many and varied religions as uniquely different trees along a thousand mile river—and appreciate that they are all nurtured by the same waters—any of us, whatever his or her variety of religious experience, should be able to see the river as the common nurturer of all our spiritual traditions and common values, without embarrassment or fear.

Yet curiously, either through indifference or cynicism, or because this is a story about the invisible inner life, we don't see this truth. Most of the news media have similarly ignored what could be the seminal story of our time. This may explain why so many journalists misunderstood or slammed the First Lady [Hillary Clinton] when she dared to touch on the subject several years ago, referring to America's "sleeping sickness of the soul."

The great challenge of our time is to live up to one of our nation's founding credos, E Pluribus Unum: out of many, one. But the feeling of unity without uniformity almost certainly will not emerge from politics or economics as we know them today. If we are truly to love one another as brothers and sisters, as children of God, we must begin to draw up some new mental maps for a new century and beyond—maps that begin to sketch out the lost continent of the human spirit: the capacity for awe, wonder, mys- tery, art, music, love, compassion, and the search for higher meaning.

I continue to believe that the American Way is both a set of values and the will to act on those values. At a time when polls show people of all ages losing enthusiasm for democracy, we must join together to ensure that our children and grandchildren grow and live in a society shaped by the deepest commitment to pluralism, individuality, freedom of thought, expression, and religion, and tolerance and compassion for one another, including the "least" among us: the economically irrelevant, the politically disenfranchised, the culturally alienated, the poor in spirit.

If not us, who? It's like the father who knocks on his son's door to shout, "Jamie, get up!" The son answers, "I don't want to get up. I don't want to go to school. And I've got three reasons. First, cause it's so hard; second, the kids all tease me; and third, I'm scared." To which the father shouts: "Now I'm gonna give you three reasons why you must go to school. First, because it's your duty; second, because you are 45 years old; and third, because you're the headmaster!"

We're all the headmasters here. The American Way resides in the conscience of millions of Americans, but it must not remain only there. Freedom of religion and spiritual quest, respect for diversity, commitment to a culture of opportunity and tolerance of complexity-these must be strengthened and safeguarded in Congress and state capitols, in libraries and classrooms, in courthouses and houses of worship, on sidewalks and in cyberspace, and in the hearts and minds of all of our fellows.

For ourselves, for the child nestled in our laps, for the child he or she may one day raise, it's too important to give up. The individual matters as never before. Together, we can strengthen the common cords that connect us as citizens, as humans, and as siblings in the Great Spirit which transcends us even as it holds us in its embrace.

The religious feeling, the burning that results in outpourings of love and commitment to our highest ideals—this is our Original Gift, which must be harnessed once more and, this time, held in place. Only this higher order can transcend our sacred tribalisms, the man-made ideologies that divide us. It is the only real source of the national reconstruction we so urgently need.

Perviz E. Randeria is an organization and management development consultant based in the San Francisco Bay Area. Her consulting assignments include large systems change processes, improvement of work processes, project management, developing cross-functional teams, effective management of work force diversity, executive and individual coaching, conflict mediation, and group facilitation. Randeria has worked as an internal consultant in a public agency and consults for both private and public-benefit organizations.

Prior to her consulting career, she was executive director of the Center for Institutional Change, an experiential education, peer learning, and community service program at San Francisco State University where she utilized her management, teaching, program design, staff development, and counseling skills.

Randeria is a member of both the National and Bay Area Organization Development Networks and served on the editorial team of *Vision Action*, the journal of the Bay Area Organization Development Network.

11

Being Different and Making a Difference

Perviz E. Randeria

Long before I became an organizational development consultant I was a little Zoroastrian girl living in Pakistan on the large, incredibly diverse continent of Asia.

Pakistan, an Islamic country, was part of India, which is predominantly Hindu, when my parents and most of my siblings were born. Our religious ancestry is ancient Persian or Zoroastrian, which is not the majority group or culture in either India and Pakistan.

For me diversity was a way of life compounded by the fact that I lived as a Zoroastrian in a predominantly Moslem culture. The people around me had similar skin color and facial features to mine but practiced a different religion, or spoke a different language, or dressed differently, or had different beliefs and values. At school my teachers were Zoroastrian, Moslem, Hindu, and Christian.

Reflecting on my experiences, I am aware that diversity is embedded in who I am. It strongly influences my thinking and actions, how I view myself, and how I relate to others. I find that knowing myself is a prerequisite for dealing and interacting with others and that I have a personal choice in how I relate or interact which can create synergy or conflict.

Now I live and work in the San Francisco Bay Area—and diversity is at least as much a way of life here as it was in Pakistan. My organizational consulting work involves helping the extraordinarily diverse individuals and groups of the Bay Area to develop effective work relationships.

My role is to create "synergy," a combined, cooperative action of independent or separate parts that results in a greater whole. Creating synergy is a challenge among like-minded people and even more so among a variety of people who contribute a multitude of life and work experiences, personal values, ways of thinking, abilities, skills, and perspectives. But synergy implies the inherent necessity of combining variety and differences for growth, creativity, and change.

I would like to share three things I have learned about how to create synergy in the midst of diversity.

First, in my organizational work, I see pervasive feelings of "us and them," feelings of powerlessness, feelings of victimization, an inability or unwillingness to take responsibility, resistance to other points of view, and difficulty in acknowledging when things are working and changing for the better. These responses come from high-level management staff as well as line staff.

I have found that the essential first step for stimulating synergy in diversity is to *create a shared understanding of the existing issues and concerns of the work group in relation to the task at hand*. This common definition requires a grasp of the different views, perspectives, and experiences of and by the people involved.

Second, in order to get working groups to discuss their perspectives on the task they wish to accomplish together, I need to *create a process in which people feel free to communicate*. People work in synergy when they have an environment in which they will be heard, understood, recognized, and validated when they share their experiences and perspectives. In a free environment, most people invariably realize that they have much in common with one another and are often surprised by this new knowledge. They come to see that the amount of time and energy they have spent on aggressively asserting strongly held views has been wasted. They understand that those overly defended views were often based on misperceptions, unchecked assumptions, or unresolved interpersonal conflicts from past interactions.

Acknowledging, addressing, and discussing the thinking behind differences and strongly held views or difficult to raise issues (usually issues of power, gender, race, competency) is essential for creating work group synergy. The experiential learning processes I use encourage people to create solutions, stimulate simultaneous attention and learning from self and others, and reinforce the interdependence of the work group or team.

Third, I have come to believe that my work of creating synergy in diversity is primarily about teaching the essential competencies needed to create synergy:

- To know how to establish boundaries, rules, and context in any situation and interaction
- To have personal awareness, accessibility, and understanding of these boundaries
- To understand personal values based upon experiences and background
- To be able and ready to explore, discuss, and work interdependently

In summary, my personal journey and experience has taught me that working together to create synergy is a process of evolution. It requires time, conscious thought, effort, commitment, persistence, humor, and forgiveness. It is more likely to happen when group members can profess shared commitment:

- To know themselves and to continually learn and be curious
- To seek a sense of the meaning and purpose of life and their interconnectedness
- To understand and accept the fact that their influence and impact upon others result from their conscious choices and their personal responsibility for those choices

The synergy in diversity that results from these ways of thinking and being are, in the end, grounded in spiritual, psychological, and personal development work and in an ongoing process of reflecting and learning from life experiences. My key learning is that my own inner work is what most enables me to help create synergy in diversity for others.

Patrick O'Neill leads Extraordinary Conversations, a Toronto-based management consulting firm specializing in leadership and organizational development.

His work in leadership education, organizational renewal, and conflict resolution has taken him to global corporations in North America and Europe, to the townships of South Africa, and to the peace process in the Middle East.

An accomplished teacher, mentor, and writer, O'Neill is committed to providing practical skills and processes that support personal and collective effectiveness, creativity, leadership, and wisdom.

With Angeles Arrien, O'Neill leads several educational programs, including "Thresholds of Collective Wisdom,", "Triumph of the Imagination," and "The Courage to Change."

O'Neill lives in Toronto with his wife, Lynne, and their three daughters, Alannah, April, and Ariana.

12

The Sangoma's Gift:
Building Inclusion Through Honor, Respect, and Generosity of Spirit

Patrick O'Neill

On a visit to South Africa, I met a man named Oswell who gave me much to ponder about honor, respect, and generosity of spirit in building inclusion. The occasion that brought us together was a three-day meeting that explored themes of forgiveness and reconciliation between black, brown, and white communities in the new South Africa.

Oswell is a Sangoma, or traditional healer, of the Xhosa people. He arrived on the first morning of the seminar with his host, an Afrikaaner named Stephen. I was asked to meet them at the door and unofficially make them welcome. It was my first meeting with a Sangoma, and I was nervous, unsure of how to greet him.

Oswell is a tall, powerfully built man in his mid-fifties. On that day he wore a gray tweed sports jacket over a T-shirt and slacks and a traditional fur hat. The Sangoma made a soft clapping motion in greeting. Instinctively, I clapped back.

As the fortunate beneficiary of a short coaching session on traditional protocol, I had been directed to ask where the Sangoma wished to be seated in the circle of participants. Oswell indicated a seat on the east side of the room, in the direction associated with the ancestors by the Xhosa people. I inquired how he wished to have his presence acknowledged in the collective. Oswell indicated that this was a question he wished to consider and that I needed to do nothing at the time.

The first day of the meeting proceeded, seemingly without incident. Oswell the Sangoma sat in his seat in the east, keenly observing the dialogue process as it unfolded, a silent participant. By day's end, however, it appeared that all was not well with the Sangoma. As he departed, Oswell confided that the traditional protocol that would have allowed him to fully participate in the collective had not been observed.

I was alarmed at this news. What protocol was he talking about? Had I not asked him what could be done to acknowledge his presence?

Oswell explained that traditional protocol required that a Sangoma be publicly acknowledged as a sign of respect and that the responsibility for acknowledgment rested with Stephen, his host. Because this had not happened, the Sangoma had been made "invisible" and without a place in the group. He had been dishonored, and the disrespect had left him feeling "unwell." Oswell told me that he would need to speak with Stephen about the matter before he returned to the meeting on the following day.

The next morning the Sangoma was back. We clapped our morning greetings to each other as he took his place in the east, opposite Stephen. At the first opportunity, Stephen rose and addressed the collective. He formally apologized to Oswell for his breach of traditional protocol and acknowledged that his act of dishonor and disrespect had left his guest "invisible" the previous day.

He explained that he had meant Oswell no harm. But in his own defense Stephen admitted that he had not possessed the knowledge of how to introduce or include a Xhosa Sangoma in a meeting. He thanked the Sangoma for allowing him to rectify the discourtesy, acknowledged him for his diplomacy and skill at bringing the matter to his attention, and apologized once more for his lack of awareness.

Then Oswell rose. He confirmed that he had been sickened by the lack of recognition and acknowledgment that had caused him to have no place in the collective. Oswell said this incident had reminded him that the traditional ways of honor and respect were rapidly disappearing. This was especially evident, he said, because the people had forgotten the importance and place of the ancestors. That the ancestors were no longer acknowledged and honored was at the root of the problem, the root cause of sickness in society. Soon, he reckoned, the Sangomas would have no place in their own culture. Then what would happen to the people?

It was easy to see from the Sangoma's point of view how the decline of honor and respect could erode a whole culture. Oswell acknowledged Stephen for correcting the breach of protocol. This would allow him, he assured the collective, a proper place to fully participate. Now he was feeling well again and looked forward to the day ahead.

The incident of the sick Sangoma caught most of us by surprise. I could see Oswell's point of view. But I could also see Stephen's and empathized with his plight as the host.

It was not that Stephen held an intention to be disrespectful of Oswell. Rather, it seemed to be a case of "disharmonic convergence"—one of those seemingly innocuous encounters between cultures that, despite good intentions, become crash sites for honor and respect.

Stephen believed that he had been a good host by inviting his friend Oswell to the meeting. He was confident that extending an invitation, providing transportation, and acting in a courteous manner were acts of good hosting. By most Western standards, Stephen was an exemplary host. By indigenous standards, he missed the boat.

The Withering of Involvement

The story of Oswell and Stephen is unfortunately widespread, played out daily in countless ways. In dialogue sessions I have witnessed hundreds of people talk about the pain and embarrassment that comes from the dishonor and disrespect they have felt. These experiences commonly fall into two broad categories of lack of appreciation: "Not Being Seen" and "Not Being Heard." When we are unseen or unheard, the message is clear: We are less worthy.

That a human being is intrinsically better, more gifted, or more worthy is an abhorrent concept to most people. This is especially true in the West, where we argue that equality is the basis of our social contract. But our behavior routinely lags behind our espoused beliefs, and this is often so with issues of diversity. Our competitive society is reductionist—people are either winners or losers. This is, as Oswell might say, a root cause of the continued decline of honor and respect between people.

We have all been on the receiving end of disrespect, and we have all dished it out. Those very same dialogue participants who shared their pain and alienation of not being seen or heard also uncovered countless examples of when they were guilty of unconscious, careless, and unskilled behavior that undermined the dignity of others. A different kind of pain went with that realization.

And yet, central to most cultures of the world is a tradition of hospitality with well-defined protocol—time-honored values, norms, skills, and behaviors assigned to the role of host and the role of guest. To violate these codes would bring dishonor to the individual, family, community, even the nation. Transgressions of honor, respect, and hospitality have often been rectified on the battlefield.

With hostilities and conflicts accelerating within and between families, organizations, communities, and nations, it would seem prudent to recover our traditional protocols and practices of hospitality. How and why did we lose them? Perhaps in the stories that we stopped telling, the songs that we no longer sing, the community rituals that have lost their meaning or have been forgotten altogether. We have, as Oswell suggests, forgotten the ancestors.

The Good Host

How can we begin to restore hospitality to ensure that our guests are honored—that they have a place from which to participate, a place to be seen and heard? One pathway is through the recovery of meaning.

The word *host* means "to extend warmth and generosity to guests or strangers." Host, hospitality, hospital, and hospice all share a common root—the Latin word *hospitia*.

Hospitality is a cornerstone of collective relationship. A good host is one who is open or receptive to another. A good host treats a guest with honesty, fairness, and respect. A good host recognizes and acknowledges the worthiness of the guest. A good host is gracious, kind, courteous, and compassionate.

The word *hostile* shares the same Latin root. Hostility is characterized by antagonism, unfriendliness, lack of warmth or generosity. Hostility is indifference. It is the arrogance of ignorance.

It is an act of hostility when we are not honored, respected, and received. It is an act of hostility to find ourselves in a culture where we are not heard or acknowledged. In these moments we move from responsibility into reactivity. From reactivity comes conflict.

In many ways Stephen was a good host to Oswell. The breakdown occurred because Stephen and Oswell did not share a common understanding of the roles and responsibilities of hospitality. Stephen was unaware of the protocols that would allow Oswell to be seen in the collective. As a result, Oswell was not acknowledged publicly by his host as a worthy person.

Hosting Gifts and Talents

Later, an astute colleague observed that while Stephen's apology had allowed Oswell to participate in the collective, the Sangoma's true gift and talent as a healer had not come forward.

It was true. The Sangoma had performed an important function as a teacher. Over the three-day meeting, Oswell had consistently provided valuable insights and observations representing traditional or indigenous perspectives. I wonder what impact the Sangoma might have made had we the sensitivity and skills to host his gifts and talents for healing. That these gifts were not available to a forum on healing the wounds of apartheid is an irony and a loss.

Oswell's plight is common. So many of the diverse individual and cultural gifts and talents that people bring into collectives and communities are placed at risk, lost, or withheld because we are poor hosts. Through ignorance, insensitivity, or lack of training, we are often reminded that there is no place for us or our gifts and talents.

Looking at this phenomena in a corporate setting, I have heard many senior executives complain that they are not getting a high enough return on their human resources, especially around issues of creativity, productivity, and problem solving.

One of the principal reasons for this, according to the people in their organizations, is the preponderance of low-trust, high-risk environments exacerbated by stress.

Stress is often rooted in the collective belief that there is insufficient time, talent, and resources to solve problems and seize opportunities. In this climate, civility is undermined by fear. To expose your gifts and talents is to be vulnerable to the judgment and evaluation of others. This presents a risk. Similarly, many people in organizations espouse the intention to honor diversity, yet practice expediency, citing the bottom line as justification: a classic Catch 22.

Inclusion: Breaking the Cycle

How do we break this cycle and restore honor and respect to daily life so that diverse cultures, perspectives, experiences, gifts, and talents are available? The biggest opportunity is the development of inclusion skills and practices. Inclusion is *the ability to actively cultivate a contribution of people's diverse gifts, talents, and experiences for the collective good.*

Many of us feel isolated and excluded from our families, communities, and organizations. We have colluded to an illusion that we do not make a difference. This illusion is supported by the common experience of not being seen or heard. Despair and alienation commonly accompany this experience.

The good host is a master of inclusion who recognizes that everyone's contribution is important to the collective well-being. The good host ignites gifts, talents, and collective wisdom by applying the skills of inclusion, especially the tools of *empathic listening* and *acknowledgment.*

Empathic Listening

Empathic listening is *the ability to set aside one's own assumptions to fully receive or include other people.* It is the ability to host different points of view and suspend judgment and evaluation of others. It is the ability to put compassion and intimacy to work in relationship.

Applying this skill may have prevented the conflict that emerged between Oswell and Stephen and supported their shared commitment to a friendship that bridged cultures.

Empathic listening has four steps.

Disarm

The first step is *to make and keep a commitment to understand others.* That is, to understand where others are coming from, what their needs are, and what unique contributions they have to offer.

To accomplish this, we must "disarm." This requires that our commitment to understand another person be equal to or greater than our commitment to our own agenda. And, we must be able to hold that commitment over those influences that may divert our attention, distract us from our role, or create defensive reasoning or behaviors.

The fears that block our ability to disarm are embarrassment and threat.

These fears are rooted in the belief that we must protect ourselves from others by hiding or covering up lest we be discovered to be somehow not good enough.

When we experience the fear of embarrassment, we seek protection or become aggressive, believing ourselves to be "under attack." These fears set in motion a dynamic of "hostility." It is virtually impossible to give and receive in relationships when we experience this form of reactivity.

In order to disarm, we must work hard to rebuild trust. When we establish safety in relationships, we can become successful at this step of empathic listening. It is useful to begin by asking ourselves some questions that will help us determine our state of readiness:

- In this conversation, what am I committed to in my role as a listener? Am I hosting the messenger? Am I hosting the message? What distracts me from my role as a listener?

- Is this a safe place for my honored guest? This is especially important when we're having conversations in which we don't share the same perspective.

- Is this a place that allows me to slow down? One of the tenets of good hosting is that we have enough time for our honored guest—that we're not trying to race through the moment to get somewhere else.

- What is the state of our relationship? Where is the trust level? What must I do to ensure that I am trustworthy?

- Have we agreed on a process for communication and especially for listening? Too much focus on the content of our message and too little on the process sabotages good listening and communication. Is there enough time for everybody to express themselves?

- Is there agreement about confidentiality? Nothing erodes trust and is more dishonorable and more disrespectful than breaking confidentiality.

- Am I being patient? Am I treating this person as though he or she is my honored guest? Am I extending kindness and courtesy?

Remembering and using these questions is fundamental to assuring the success of the first step of empathic listening—to disarm.

The challenge for Oswell and Stephen at this step of empathic listening was to work together so that the *personal* and the *cultural* assumptions accompanying the roles and responsibilities of hospitality were mutually understood. This promotes safety. Stephen would know what was expected of him as host because it would have been agreed. Unfortunately, the conversation did not take place perhaps because the second step of empathic listening was not observed.

Suspend Assumptions

The second step of empathic listening is *to create an opening by suspending our assumptions.* Assumptions are the stories, pictures, preconceptions, beliefs, and patterns that we hold as true without testing them out.

Because we have come to identify with these assumptions so completely, they form the filters through which we understand and know the world. This process is automatic and self-sealing, leaving us unaware of the impact our assumptions have on our perceptions of reality and our receptivity to other people.

In the geography of our psyche, assumptions are like "tectonic plates," a rigidity associated with the formation of land masses. Just as the earth transforms from liquid to solid states, so do our perceptions. They can become fixed and static, creating an over-identification or attachment with one location on our perceptual map. This sets up the conditions for the human dynamics that accompany fixed perspectives and inflexibility.

The meaning of the word *respect* is "to look again." By suspending our assumptions, we recover the ability to extend respect, to look again. This creates an opening for another person to be seen and understood on his or her own terms, not on our own rigid or fixed terms.

We don't have to give up our beliefs to suspend our assumptions. We simply set them to one side so we can receive what another has to offer without the filter of automatic, preconceived, personal, and cultural conditioning. This allows us greater flexibility, more flow, and the opportunity to view experience through the eyes of other people.

As a result, we can appreciate and host different points of view and extend true generosity of spirit to others. Ultimately, we may learn something from the perspectives or experiences of other people, causing us to modify our viewpoints and grow.

Suspending our assumptions reduces the collisions that can occur when the tectonic plates of differing perceptions meet. The fault lines of diversity give way to a natural convergence that enriches everyone.

Four questions have proven useful as a way of interrupting the automatic nature of assumptions:

- What if how I see it is not true?
- What if the opposite is true?
- What if it's half true?
- What if it's only true for me?

Asking these four questions helps interrupt our perceptual and behavioral patterns for reflection. This creates an opening where it is possible to suspend our assumptions and fully receive another person.

Suspending our assumptions may be one of our most challenging hosting skills. Had the second skill of empathic listening been applied to the case of the sick Sangoma, it could have prevented the experience of "dis-ease" for both Oswell and Stephen.

Stephen assumed that Oswell's needs were met. As a result, Stephen was surprised to find himself in conflict with Oswell without the awareness of what he had done to contribute to the situation.

To practice the skill of suspending assumptions, Stephen could have asked Oswell, "Is there something I could be doing to support your participation in the meeting?"

Oswell could have replied, "There are some traditional protocols that need to be observed by both of us. Here's what they are. Thank you for asking."

The ability to suspend our assumptions and interrupt the automatic nature of how we see and respond to the world is vital to creating an opening for diversity. It prepares us for step three—hosting our honored guests.

Put Feelings First, Facts Second

The third step is to remember to *"host" the messenger and the message as honored guests, acknowledging feelings first and facts second.* By hosting the messenger, we extend honor and respect, recognizing that person as a human being with feelings and not just as a "task delivery system." We also pay respectful attention to the content of the message. This is an authentic act of hospitality.

Because this is empathic listening—the listening skill that creates safety and trust through empathy—it is important that the human connection be established by hosting feelings first. We act on the intention of putting our guest at ease, providing a safe place to disarm. When people's feelings are acknowledged, it signals the importance that is placed on the person and on the relationship. This provides a solid foundation for working together and establishes the relationship line between people. Authenticity and congruence is the glue that bonds the line.

This is the skill that served Stephen and Oswell well in the process of reconciliation. When Stephen acknowledged Oswell's feelings, he demonstrated his commitment to the individual, his friendship, and a deep respect for the position Oswell held within his community. This allowed a correction to take place in the relationship, recovering the balance that had been upset by Stephen's unintentional discourtesy.

Often, we come together cautiously, fearful of exposing ourselves to threat or embarrassment that could lead to loss of face and hostility.

This third skill of empathic listening is particularly useful in diversity situations because "creative tension" is usually present as people look for bridges across personal and cultural gaps.

Empathic listening acknowledges or "hosts" how people are feeling—it acknowledges the fears and sensitivities that accompany the unknown in relationship. This allows us to slow down and take the time necessary for *familiarity*, which comes from the Latin *familiaritas*, the root word of *family* and *intimacy*. Hosting feelings first results in safety, promotes learning, and supports friendship and collegiality.

We deal with "facts second" to convey our understanding of the message. When we host the message as an honored guest, we bring all of our resources to bear on *understanding*—being "thoroughly familiar" and "coming into a state of cooperation and tolerance" with someone or something.

This is the domain of accuracy, especially vital to intercultural communication and conflict resolution. Meaning is embedded in a shared understanding of cultural and personal assumptions. As we attempt to bridge cultural gaps, where people may be working in second or third languages, it is critical to agree on what things mean. This requires precision, specificity, and patience.

Patience is an act of generosity of spirit and confirms that we are willing to devote our undivided time and attention to ensure that we move forward together in common understanding.

Understanding the messenger and the message is essential to diversity work. It promotes shared meaning, collaborative problem solving, wise management of ideas and processes, and cooperative action. This helps reduce the incidence of conflict and supports peace between people and communities.

Check In

The fourth step is *to check in to make sure that we understand the perspective of others*. Being certain of how accurately we have heard is the most important of the four steps—and it's the step we consistently forget. Why? Because most of us assume that we are skilled at listening for accuracy. Unfortunately, this assumption is often not supported by the evidence. The fourth step of empathic listening requires that we check in with the other person to make sure that what we heard is what was said.

This step is especially useful in diversity work to support the development of shared understanding and meaning across cultures.

Meaning is embedded in cultural and personal assumptions, including language, customs, myths, and group and personal experiences.

Checking in requires that we do the ground work to ensure common understanding by slowing down our communication process and discovering that what *we think we heard* and what *was meant by the speaker* are aligned. Because our minds move from particulars to generalizations at lightening speed, our reliability as listeners and speakers must always be supported by reality checks.

When Oswell first arrived at the meeting and was asked how he wished to have his presence acknowledged, he replied that he wished to consider the question further and that nothing needed to be done at the time. One might have interpreted this to mean "you're off the hook." Another interpretation is "please check in with me later."

A good host sees to the needs of the honored guest not just upon arrival. Good hospitality, like friendship, requires ongoing attention. Employing this principle, Stephen would have made a point of ensuring that Oswell's needs and concerns were met by checking in with his guest periodically throughout the course of the meeting.

Consistent checking allows us to determine how well we have practiced the first three steps of the empathic listening process. This last step is the most important because it acts as a safety net in relationship. Should we forget to *disarm, suspend our assumptions,* and *host the messenger and the message,* the skill of *checking in* with our honored guest will remind us of our commitment to empathic listening.

Acknowledgment

The companion skill to empathic listening is acknowledgment, *the conversational skill of taking notice or expressing appreciation.*

Acknowledgment is the speaking that generates inclusion— actively cultivating people's involvement by recognizing that their presence and contributions are important.

In South Africa, this is part of the "ubuntu ethic," which holds that "a person is a person because of other people." By ignoring or withholding acknowledgment, we render people invisible and limit their potential for full participation in the life of our collectives. This was the source of Oswell's sickness at the meeting. The remedy was Stephen's acknowledgment, restoring Oswell's voice in the collective.

Practicing the skill of acknowledgment is an act of healing. Yet, the widespread condition of low self-esteem would indicate that it is a healing practice in decline. We have underdeveloped and underutilized our skills of acknowledgment. Instead, we have elevated criticism to an art form.

"Wherever people receive the least acknowledgment," Dr. Angeles Arrien says, "is where they may carry beliefs of inadequacy, or low self-worth."

Acknowledgment works with empathic listening to create a safe and supportive container for our gifts and talents. The practice of these two skill sets cultivate inclusion and support diversity.

Conclusion

Oswell and Stephen recovered the balance in their relationship because they were honorable men. Their commitment to respect and generosity of spirit was greater than their commitment to being right or saving face.

The good will demonstrated by each man allowed *reconciliation*. It began when Oswell approached Stephen privately with his concerns. The respectful guest, wishing to avoid a moment of public embarrassment for his host, used discretion to bring forward information about the breach in hospitality. This was not to cover up what had happened. Rather, he sought to avoid igniting further reactivity and restore hospitality where it had been forgotten.

Stephen, acting as the good host, listened carefully to his honored guest, acknowledging both feelings and facts. He took responsibility for restoring Oswell's full participation in the collective by publicly acknowledging his oversight and praising Oswell for his patience and skill at handling the discourtesy.

The foundation for taking full advantage of and celebrating diversity in our lives is trust. Central to building trust is the practice of honor and respect. Trust and diversity are interconnected. In place they create magic. When missing, as happens so often in modern society, they create reactivity and conflict.

By returning to the practices of inclusion, we have an opportunity to recover honor and respect in relationship and as a result solve many of the issues that plague our nations, communities, companies, families, and everyday lives.

Inclusion is the protocol that allowed the Sangoma to participate in the meeting. Inclusion is also the protocol that can begin to allow each person's gifts and talents to "show up" and make a unique contribution to the collective.

Jacqueline Haessly offers Toward Inclusiveness workshops and seminars for business and organizational leaders through her business, Peacemaking Associates. Her work has appeared in more than a hundred national and international publications as well as several business anthologies, including *When the Canary Stops Singing: Women's Perspectives for Transforming Business*, *Rediscovering the Soul of Business*, and *The New Bottom Line*. Her book, *Learning to Live Together*, offers creative ways to honor and celebrate diversity in our world. For her work in peace and global awareness, she has been recognized in more than 20 volumes of *Who's Who*, including *Who's Who in International Leaders*, *2000 Notable Women*, and *Women in the Midwest*. Haessly is currently pursuing a doctoral degree from the Union Institute. When she isn't writing or teaching, she enjoys sailing, swimming, knitting, crewel, mysteries, and leading cooperative games for business and intergenerational groups. She and her husband, Dan Di Domizio, share the joy, love, tears, and laughter of busy family life.

A Journey Toward Inclusion

Jacqueline Haessly

Issues surrounding affirmative action, equal opportunity, and political correctness headline the news, providing abundant fodder for daily conversation and the seemingly endless speeches of political candidates. Diversity training in business is suspect, the subject of much debate. Much current conversation reflects a polarization of ideas—and peoples—into two dramatically different camps: those for and those against affirmative action and equal opportunity. Indeed, the terms themselves have become battle cries in today's march for equality for all citizens. What is often missing in these conversations is a basic understanding of opposing positions and a willingness to accord even minimal respect to the hearing of those positions.

Desperately needed is a willingness to address issues of social, political, and economic transformation grounded in a deep awareness of and commitment to basic human rights and human dignity. Also needed is a willingness to address these complex issues from a perspective grounded on ethical, moral, and spiritual values. Such a perspective informs issues of accessibility, that all might have opportunity to share in the goods, resources, and services available. Affirmative action, equal opportunity for all, and respect for diversity are, first of all, about living and acting with basic respect and common decency for the rights and dignity of others so that all might have equal opportunity to develop to their full potential. Indeed, genuine politically correct acts—as distinct from those which are politically expedient—flow from deeply held principles of care for the common good. As women and men of all racial, cultural, religious, and ethnic backgrounds, ages, and ability levels seek full participation in the governance of their world and benefit from the economic and political activity of their society, questions of who will benefit and who will not rise to the surface for all.

Much of the problem in our society can be traced to our "isms": racism, sexism, ageism, classism, nationalism, heterosexualism, homosexualism, among others. Each "ism" impacts on both the personal and the public levels of our lives. At the personal level, the internalization of beliefs and attitudes affect how we view each other and relate to each other in our families, neighborhoods, workplaces, and world. At the public level, these attitudes and beliefs are institutionalized in our government, education, and business policies, practices, and programs. When such policies and practices based on gender, skin color, cultural and religious differences, age or ability level, or some other criteria are institutionalized, it leads to exclusion; the uneven and unfair distribution of power and resources; and the establishment of laws and policies which favor one group over another. We will all benefit from a deeper understanding of these social, political, and economic policies and practices that impact society and that lead to the current unrest.

How might we as a society address any problems that flow from these "isms" and impact how well we relate to the diversity of peoples who share life with us on this planet? This essay offers five stages for addressing this issue: (1) becoming aware, (2) naming the problem, (3) deepening our understanding, (4) taking action, and (5) celebrating our diversity. Each in turn will lead to a greater appreciation of the similarities and differences we each bring to the common experiences of our shared humanity.

Becoming Aware

My personal interest in the issue of stereotypes and exclusion began in childhood. When I was about eight, there was a young girl who lived several blocks from our home. She was deaf and spoke in a way that was often difficult to understand unless one listened attentively. During the summer we often played on the same playground. Many of the children and some adults taunted and teased her because of her poor speech. I had been taught that it was cruel to laugh at people with physical handicaps, so I didn't laugh at her. What I hadn't learned was how to be her friend. Because I didn't want to risk the teasing that might have been turned on me if I had dared to play with her, I didn't befriend her. I failed to understand that to ignore or avoid her was also cruel. I didn't realize then that I, too, was handicapped because of this limitation caused by fear. Today, I know that both of us were poorer because I feared to honor her differences and failed to welcome her as a unique person in my life.

There are many other examples from my childhood when fear of a person's race, economic class, or a family's medical condition kept me from reaching out to welcome and embrace others who were different from members of my family or me. There were times, too, when I or a member of my family experienced the pain of exclusion. On each of those occasions, we all lost the opportunity to share something special in our lives.

My professional interest in this topic came out of my experiences while serving on a subcommittee for the Milwaukee Board of School Directors in 1970. This subcommittee was responsible for examining children's reading textbooks to determine how well they helped children develop reading skills. What I soon discovered was that no matter how well the textbooks might have been designed to teach reading skills, they also communicated other messages that were disturbing. Pictures and texts revealed subtle messages reflecting widely held cultural beliefs about roles and lifestyles of whole groups of people: women of all races, men of color, the elderly, and those differently abled, among others. I began examining textbooks from other subjects: math, science, social studies, language arts, music and, in religious schools, religion. There, too, the pattern was similar. I discovered that textbooks, meant to teach one curriculum, frequently introduced students to another, much more subtle curriculum, one that often reflected gender, racial, and cultural stereotyping and patterns of exclusion.

Naming the Problem

The Classroom Perspective: Children's Textbooks and the Subtle Curriculum

The patterns found in children's textbooks suggest that schools, in the business of educating society's young for leadership for the next generation, unintentionally pass on messages far different from those intended. While children's textbooks may provide information and aid in skill development in specific subject areas, thoughtful educators and parents recognize that textbooks do much more than this. Among other things, they provide a framework by which students are introduced to important concepts about society and its people. All too often, these concepts are communicated in pictures and text that also convey a message about who can and should do something based on age, culture, gender, national origin, or racial characteristics. I name this pattern the subtle curriculum.

The subtle curriculum involves both role stereotyping and patterns of exclusion. Role stereotyping examines how people are portrayed, either in pictures, text or both. It includes all forms of stereotyping based on gender, age, race, ethnicity, culture, nationality, religious heritage, political persuasion, sexual orientation, class, and lifestyle choices. Role stereotyping occurs whenever individuals or groups of people are assigned a specific type of role and are seldom portrayed in any other way.

Examples of role stereotyping include women portrayed only in nurturing roles as mothers and homemakers or in caregiving roles as nurses and teachers; Euro-American men portrayed in business suits as authority figures in government, medicine, law, or in uniforms as police officers or fire fighters; men of color portrayed as mechanics and laborers; families of color portrayed as recipients of social services; boys engaged in active play; girls receiving assistance from boys or fathers; elderly people portrayed on park benches feeding bread crumbs to the pigeons or as people in need of assistance; and those with disabilities portrayed as receivers of care, if they are portrayed at all.

Patterns of exclusion occur when children's textbooks fail to include certain groups, such as minorities, the elderly, or the handicapped actively participating in the ordinary life of a community. Patterns of exclusion occur in two ways. Whole groups of people or cultures might be excluded from a body of work. More often, racial or cultural groups are included, but are limited in the ways they are portrayed. Patterns of exclusion are more subtle and pervasive, as well as more difficult to identify or acknowledge than patterns based on role stereotypes. Discovering them depends upon the questions one asks!

Examples of patterns of exclusion include minority families portrayed only in social studies texts or readers that deal with minority issues, such as congestion in urban tenements or the life of migrant workers; disabled people pictured only in health books or social studies books in units on health; men and boys of any race or culture seldom, if ever, shown in nurturing and caregiving roles. In many children's textbooks, women, men of color, and people with differing ability levels are seldom portrayed as members of the general population contributing in meaningful ways as scientists, physicians, professors, manufacturers, or government leaders. Their stories are seldom fully developed.

Patterns of exclusion also become evident through an examination of the indexes of most textbooks, grade school through graduate school. Often, these indexes, indicating whose ideas are considered important and whose are left out, reveal a lopsided view of history, leaving out the contributions of most women as well as men of color.

If children's math, reading, music, English or social studies textbooks do not portray women or men of African, Asian, Native American, and Hispanic heritage in professional roles, in positions of community responsibility, or in leadership positions, neither children nor teachers might notice, unless of course they happened to be from a minority group. If the spelling, social studies, or science books fail to include pictures of the elderly, the handicapped, or minority groups actively engaged in careers or the everyday activities of ordinary life, who would miss them? Who will care? The answer is, we all should!

These are just a few of the more classic examples of role stereotyping and patterns of exclusion that unfortunately continue to occur in some children's textbooks even though there has been effort made to correct some stereotypes. When such images are reinforced day after day and year after year, readers begin to believe them. Those who see themselves in positions of control and dominance, as actors in the events of human history, forget about those who are excluded, or worse, believe the image and continue the patterns of exclusion in their own life and work. People who are excluded or limited in their options begin to think that they have no alternatives, that there is no place for them in our society. This is a violence of exclusion that destroys a part of the humanity in all of us. In the end everyone loses.

The Business Perspective: Media, Business, and the Perpetuation of Exclusion

As a result of my work with these textbooks, I developed a two-part workshop series for educators, parents, and leaders in business and community organizations. Part one, "Uncovering the Subtle Curriculum," includes a review and analysis of children's textbooks and other print and visual media. Part two, "Toward Inclusiveness," provides opportunities for participants to examine the patterns of discrimination in their own lives and begin to break through these patterns. One unexpected result of this work of textbook analysis has developed into an occupational hazard that creeps—uninvited—into much of my personal or professional reading and other dimensions of my life. Halfway through my reading of an article, viewing television or videos, or even when listening to a presentation, I begin to fidget, my mind will stray, and other unmistakable signs of restlessness alert me. Rather than pay attention to the message that was intended, I find myself aware of a subtler message, one that is unintentionally communicated by the inclusion or exclusion of an important word or phrase, what I have come to call the "case of the missing word" syndrome.

I've discovered that writers and illustrators of children's textbooks are not alone in using language and pictures that contain messages far different from those intended. Nor is the effect of this subtle curriculum limited to our children's classrooms. Examples can be found in bestselling business books and magazines; our local, regional, and national news publications; movies; television and cable news programs, documentaries and entertainment; advertising; and the audiovisual training materials used in our places of business. They permeate our society and creep insidiously and often unintentionally into our personal lives as well as our professional work through our written and spoken words, our research, our training programs, our marketing, and our business and leadership conferences. A few examples selected from college textbooks, trade publications, and conference brochures reveal the prevalence of such patterns within the world of business.

- An undergraduate level economics textbook includes references to 203 people in the index; only 6 are women. Since women have addressed significant economic issues at policy levels and at the level of community development, this is a serious omission.

- The index of a popular textbook for business managers at the graduate level includes 187 references to people; 18 are to women. We must ask ourselves what message trainees in business management receive by this exclusion of women's voices.

- A textbook for a course on advertising portrays people in limited, stereotypical roles: Women extol the value of home care products and appliances while men promote sports, lawn, and car care equipment; men and women with beautiful bodies enjoy fine cars, wines and liquors, or fantasy vacations. In this particular textbook, no ads portrayed people with gray hair, or people with obvious physical disabilities, except for one ad that showed a person in a wheelchair using a home health-care product. The obvious message was that women care for the home and provide its services, men engage in sports and care for the lawn and car, while people who are older, have gray hair, weigh more, or need assistance with physical care do not drive cars, wear clothing, enjoy fine food and drink, or vacation like the rest of society.

- A survey of the indexes of bestselling business books aimed at managers and leaders in the world of business and often used in managerial courses reveals how widespread this pattern of exclusion is. Readers who do their own survey of some of these bestselling books for business managers and leaders will discover that few indexes of these books include the names of women or men of color. With few exceptions, this renders them almost invisible in the world of business.

Numerous magazines written today identify a specific gender as their target group. Readers therefore expect women's magazines to feature articles and even use language that is specific to women. Men's magazines do likewise. However, there are also numerous magazines written on topics of concern to both women and men. These include business, education, psychology, science, and other magazines that appeal to special interest groups without regard to gender. How well do these publications reflect awareness of and sensitivity to issues of gender, race, and ethnic and cultural diversity?

- A popular business magazine aimed at entrepreneurs recently included numerous feature articles about successful men and only one small article about eight successful women. Photographs that accompanied the articles included fifty-seven white men, two minority men, and eight women.

- One three-part essay in a major international publication addressed the impact of war and violence on international business. The author included references to ninety-three people, including government, business, and religious leaders, politicians, scientists, scholars, poets, essayists, novelists, and artists. Only six of the ninety-three people named were women, yet women's voices have been at the forefront in all cultures addressing this topic.

- A magazine promoting quality in writing included the phrase, "Bonnie, Roy, and two black guys from Boston." What color, I wondered, were Bonnie and Roy! Why *was* it important to mention the color of skin for the men from Boston but not for the other two people in the story? What did *that* information add to the story? And, I wondered to myself, did the black men have names? Further on in the essay, the author mentions his friend Tony, his car Molly, and his wife—all in one sentence, with no name given for his wife. The irony is that this particular essay was titled "Putting Humanity into One's Writing."

A cursory glance at the promotional materials for professional business conferences and training events also reveals how deeply embedded these patterns of exclusion are in the world of business.

- A national conference, "Quality of Work for the Future," included eighty workshops; only two women were listed as presenters.

- A five-day regional conference, "Jobs for the Future," offered a selection of three workshop tracks of twenty workshops each; each workshop lasted the entire five days. In addition there were three luncheon speakers and a daily keynoter. Only two of the sixty presenters in the entire five days were woman, one a luncheon moderator. Only one person of color was included as a presenter. All of the photos in the brochure were of white men.

- A Midwest regional business conference included one hundred workshops. Five were offered by women, including one by a Hispanic woman. Eight were offered by minority men. All five keynoters were white men. The conference brochure highlighted four of the keynoters and the two female entertainers.

- The national conference of a major professional organization included eighty workshops and four keynote speakers. All of the keynoters were white men. Twelve of the workshop presenters were white women; three people were members of minority groups. All ten photos in the four-color promotional brochure were of white men.

The not-for-profit sector, too, is sometimes remiss in seeking to reflect inclusiveness in program planning and accessibility.

- A week-long regional housing conference included seven keynote speakers, one of whom was a woman and none of whom was a minority, even though issues of accessible housing significantly affect these populations disproportionately.

- Keynoters at a national conference on social issues included twelve men and two women in the first three days of the five-day conference. Both women were part of a panel presentation while only two of the twelve men were part of a panel. One woman scheduled to speak canceled at the last moment due to a family emergency. She was replaced by a white male, even though a woman who had worked at the executive level of that organization and was a noted speaker was also present at the conference.

- All major conference events for a national professional organization, including general assemblies, workshops, and meals, were held in locations that were not handicapped accessible, thus preventing persons with disabilities from attending.

This is just a small sampling of the hundreds of promotional brochures and conference programs that cross my desk each month. Minority women and men are, at times, included as presenters in conferences that address critical minority issues in large urban areas, issues such as poverty, crime, education, and drugs. But one must seek far to find minorities represented in business and organizational conferences addressing a broader spectrum of human concerns and human endeavors.

Television advertising, news shows, documentaries, and video training materials provide other opportunities to reflect inclusiveness in our society. However, advertising for television and cable programming continues to perpetuate role stereotypes, often based on gender or ability level. Moderators of nightly or weekly news documentaries continue to come under fire for their habit of consistently interviewing white males as *the* experts for most national and international events. Seldom are white women or people of color included as equals in the role of expert. Instead, their inclusion on any program is often as victim or as the cause of pressing social problems. Training videos developed within organizations, as well as those developed for organizations by outside experts, also reflect a limited view of who does what and how. Many such videos include no people of color or do so in ways that portray people in stereotypical roles.

Some may be tempted to ask, Why all the fuss? Why do we need gender, age, racial, ethnic, and cultural diversity or inclusive language in our places of work, our brochures, our literature, our presentations, even our boards? The answer is simple. The task of the businessperson is to generate business for one's company through the communication of an idea, the sale of a product, or delivery of a service. To do so effectively requires that managers, employees, customers, suppliers, and communities believe in themselves and in each other, believe that their voices matter. When people engaged in the daily activities of business use generic language patterns such as *man* for humanity, *he* for women and men—patterns that habitually exclude women, who make up more than half of the human race—women listeners feel the exclusion and injustice that is perpetrated upon them. When workplaces, brochures, newsletters, programs, or conferences contain words or photo images that exclude, even unintentionally, whole groups of people of diverse races, ethnic backgrounds, or cultures who are actually a part of a company's potential employee, supplier, or customer base, why would such people want to consider employment with that company, seek to use its services, or purchase its products?

Thus, every person's world view is adversely affected when textbooks, training manuals, trade magazines, business books, and professional conferences do not reflect the diversity that enriches our human experience.

"Who is missing?" is a question each of us as business leaders, workers, and conference planners needs to address if we are truly concerned about quality programs in our organization and in research and program development. It is our responsibility to reach out beyond our own boundaries to discover the richness that people of other races, cultures, genders, or ability levels can contribute to our organization, program, or cause. Only then will we all benefit.

Deepening Our Understanding

Business leaders concerned about problems resulting from discrimination will benefit by examining three forums for addressing the problem.

The first involves work-related situations where problems of racism, sexism, ageism, and other forms of discriminatory behaviors—whether subtle, overt or covert—occur. Business leaders have responded to workplace discrimination by providing programs on diversity training. There are two types of programs. The first stresses tasks. The second stresses attitudes that lead to changes in behavior. Task-focused training encourages workers to work together to accomplish tasks but may not change their attitudes and behaviors outside the workplace. According to Clarence Williams, founder of Recovery from Racism workshops, this is because "such training aims for tolerance and the elimination of bigotry from the work site for the sake of production and not persons." This can lead to repressed feelings of resentment and behaviors that block or frustrate productivity. Educator and author bell hooks states that "participants in diversity training find themselves faced with limitations of their knowledge of other cultures, lack of awareness of the real history of the slave trade and colonialism, and the legacy these have left on descendants— both those engaged in the practice of slavery or colonizing, and those enslaved and colonized. Indeed, exposing ourselves to such truths and uncovering both personal and social biases can be fraught with danger, often leading to confusion, chaos, and even confrontation." Her suggestion echoes those of others who claim that true liberation can only be accomplished when one has a place to tell one's story and be heard.

Diversity training that invites participants to explore their own attitudes and helps them identify common experiences goes beyond task orientation and helps people begin to examine those experiences from the vantage point of different perspectives and voices. Multicultural education is another means of bringing to the institutional forum a multiplicity of voices. Such programs invite participants to question whose voice is included or missing in the conversation. Here, though, Clarence Williams points out a flaw in multicultural programming. According to Williams, "multicultural programming can lead to the appreciation of other people's stories and cultures while neglecting to support policies which would assure their presence in our communities and our lives." Joseph Barndt, who offers "Dismantling Racism" workshops, suggests that multiculturalism is an institutional response to having more "colorful" institutions with no change in policy, practice, or program. Going further, bell hooks states, "In retrospect, I see that in the last twenty years I have encountered many folks who say they are committed to freedom and justice for all even though the way they live, the values and habits of being they institutionalize daily, in public and private rituals, help maintain the culture of domination, help create an unfree world." This is the real problem of institutionalized discriminatory practices. Even people who want to live their lives justly find the burden of changing the way they live their lives discomforting.

The second forum has to do with institutional discrimination that is reflected in the public policies, practices, and programs that affect our educational, financial, religious, business, and government bodies. It is important to name the evil that is institutionalized as sexism, racism, ageism, or other forms of discrimination, for that is the only way to uncover the stereotypes that shape our policies and our practices in all these institutions.

The third forum has to do with our personal and interpersonal relations with family, friends, neighbors, colleagues, coworkers, and strangers. How do we see ourselves in relation to people differing from ourselves? Can we acknowledge our differences and see below the surface of a person to the beauty that lies within? Can we distinguish between respect for a person and possible disagreement with that person's (or group's) attitudes, values, beliefs, or patterns of behavior? Truly effective programs that focus on respect for diversity empower people in the process of making links between their professional roles and their personal lives so that the problems identified by bell hooks are truly overcome!

Each of us detracts from or contributes to a sense of inclusiveness in our communities, our workplaces, and our world by behaviors that ignore new people or welcome them into our lives, discourage or invite conversation with those different from ourselves, limit our connections to our known group, or lead to expanding connections in a manner that embraces all. The welcoming session for new workers, organizational members, or conference attendees is one visible means of reaching out with an attitude of inclusivity. Beyond that each person must respond in a personal way to assure that others feel welcomed, valued, and included.

Taking Action

So, what *can* thoughtful business leaders and program planners do to counter this subtle curriculum and the stereotyping and patterns of exclusion they foster in the workplace? We have seen that becoming aware, naming the problem, and deepening our understanding of the complexity of the problem are preludes to taking action.

The next step is to take responsible action. According to bell hooks, "Many, wanting to engage in dialogue about diversity, find themselves uncertain as to how to proceed, how to get beyond the 'stumbling for the right words' stage."

Business leaders who appreciate the value of diversity in their workplace as well as in their communities and our world can do much to help in moving to this next stage. There are two dimensions for their actions. The first has to do with the promotion of diversity within the worksite setting itself. Business leaders can:

- promote brainstorming sessions in the workplace to identify effective ways to increase respect for diversity
- provide educational materials that offer a broader, inclusive, and holistic perspective of all peoples' contributions to society (art offers one way to do this in workplace settings)
- examine hiring and promotion practices to assure that they reflect both legal and ethical commitments to diversity in the workplace
- support the development of advertising, marketing, and training materials that reflect diverse populations
- encourage nominations to committees and boards to reflect the cultural, racial, and gender balance companies and organizations profess to desire

- refuse to support training programs that induce blame and guilt, which often leads to defensiveness and paranoia
- participate in and encourage others to participate in diversity training sessions that address issues related to both task and attitudinal change

Deep change in our society will only occur if we, as business leaders, move beyond these steps. We can do this by inviting people into the process of sharing their stories in a way that allows each one to discover common experiences—gently, so real growth takes place, and genuine personal and societal change can occur. Here, bell hooks reminds us that this "must be a place for safety and commitment to honest and open sharing of both the pain and the struggle. In such a space experiences can be shared; fears can be voiced; and hopes, dreams, and images of a more inclusive world of work and play can be expressed without fear of retaliation." She adds, "If we really want to create a cultural climate where biases can be addressed and challenged and changed, all border crossings must be seen as valid and legitimate." When women and men in the workplace gather and share their stories of pain and struggle as well as joy in an atmosphere of respect and trust, they add important insights for business leaders and workers seeking to respond with dignity, justice, and compassion about this important topic. More than anything else, such stories open our eyes, our ears, our minds, and our hearts to see what manner of people we are and who we can become.

Celebrating Our Diversity

People the world over flock to places of beauty: gardens and meadows of flowers, majestic mountains, breathtaking canyons, calming seas, and thunderous oceans. We marvel at the display of wildflowers, the glimmering fish of the sea, and the awe-inspiring beauty of a rain forest with its thousands of species of birds and plants. In all this, we sing praise for the wondrous sights and marvelous variety of beauty in our lives. Can we also find in our hearts a sense of wonder about the marvelous diversity of people who inhabit our planet, work with us in our businesses, study in our schools, enjoy our recreational activities, and share the tears, joy, love, and laughter of life with family and friends in the rural and urban communities of our world? It is this that is needed if we are to truly create a society where our difference are honored, our diversity treasured, and the communal bonds of our shared humanity celebrated. This is the task we face on our shared journey toward inclusion.

Sylvia Lafair is co-director of Creative Energy Options and works with her husband and partner, Herb Kaufman. They have developed the Sankofa Method, a model for personal and professional growth.

Sankofa, an African word, means "heal the past to free the present." It helps explain one of the themes basic to the CEO philosophy: that you can go home again—to rebalance, to rectify, to put your life and your life experience in a different order. The Sankofa philosophy looks at life from a whole systems perspective.

Dr. Lafair has worked as a family therapist and as a consultant with children and youth agencies, school districts, and corporations for more than twenty-five years. She has been an instructor at Hahnemann University, the Family Institute of Philadelphia, and the Institute for Transpersonal Psychology. She is a charter member of the American Family Therapy Academy and a supervisor for the American Association of Marriage and Family Therapists.

14

The Inside Out Project: Diversity and the Human Psyche

Sylvia Lafair

In this technical, information age, the need for process groups to share their human creative sides is vital for balance. One only has to watch the brilliant Godfrey Reggio film *Koyaanisqatsi* to consider what happens when our lives become machine motivated. *Koyaanisqatsi* in the Hopi language means life out of balance. We have only to drive through any urban area to see this word in action. When we no longer permit nature to be available to us to mirror the beauty of our own inner nature, when we reject the substance of human caring readily available yet often unaccessed in our work as well as in our home environments, and when we prefer computer games and television to exploring music or art or drama, we have created a life out of balance.

It is not easy to help a company examine its existing culture and understand its balance. The potential for backlash is huge. In this case, eighteen highly trained managers had been meeting for six months in a pilot project about diversity. While lip service was given to concerns about working with the deeper human dimensions of diversity, there was still a superficial politeness about sharing real feelings. Everyone knew the pockets of silence that occurred during the meeting were politically correct moments of caution. As of yet few had the courage to say in the group what was being said in smaller clusters behind closed doors.

The two facilitators of the program had been moving on a clear steady course to access deeper truths from the group, truths that would break down barriers and free creativity. Building trust is a complex process. Helping people trust someone they view as "different" means finding a shared language, a common denominator to move situations forward. They had spent the previous months clearing the ground so that secondary process thoughts, the ones we think yet rarely speak, could find voice. They knew the foundation had to be solid enough to support the cultural and personal loyalty ties of the collective members. The foundation had to be strong enough to contain the beliefs, hurts, shames, and longings, the invisible loyalties handed down from generation to generation that permeated the room in subtle and tangible ways. Dialogue about people, places, and situations had to be held in a sure, safe manner so that seeds of trust could be captured, planted, and nurtured.

This diversity program was a challenging experiment in a five-year-old communications company whose parent corporation was a conservative European-based veteran celebrating 108 years of business. The American-based firm was growing rapidly, and multicultural issues were demanding a new form of attention. Inside the firm there were major concerns about fairness among the races and the sexes, as well as unresolved difficulties between the parent company and its offspring about policies and procedures.

Until now the monthly day-long meetings had been designed as lessons in collective awareness. They were didactic sessions, teaching a dialogic model of communication and team-building skills to a group of highly trained technical people, products of a computer-driven era where machines could communicate individual wants and needs without so much as a human connection for days or even weeks. Voice mail, e-mail, fax machines, answering machines and now, the web, have changed the face of dialogue.

The upside of this communication revolution is that it offers the opportunity for getting the daily tactical aspects of relating out of the way so that time together can be seen as precious, can be spent in pursuit of deeper meaning and higher creative possibilities.

Product quotas, meeting agendas, new client leads, and such can be efficiently handled in short computer-driven commentaries. Issues of equal opportunities at all levels of management; concerns about balancing family time and work time; designing new and creative projects; voicing the hopes, hurts, and dreams of the individuals who congregate to create the corporate culture—these areas are better suited for times of discussion and dialogue.

The premise of the present year-long diversity program was to guide people past the statistics, past the polarities, past the known world of discussion to the powerful healing arena of dialogue. In looking at diversity issues, the group was also being given an opportunity to search for meaning and balance in their daily lives. The program has developed from the dialogic models that have been brought forward by world-renowned physicist David Bohm and the teachings of anthropologist Gregory Bateson. The content of the training has its roots in the works of renowned intergenerational family therapists Murray Bowen and Ivan Boszormenyi-Nagy. The essence of the program calls forward the wisdom of the indigenous peoples and their knowledge about collectives and the connectedness of all life, especially the work of contemporary indigenous teacher, Angeles Arrien.

The combination of dialogue, rectification work, and ancient wisdom spiced with experiential learning processes using expressive arts, breathwork, imagery, and meditation has culminated in the creation of the Sankofa Method. *Sankofa* is a Nigerian word that means heal the past to free the present. Part of our evolutionary responsibility is to become observers of our life patterns, choose those that serve us, and release the rest. We are no longer bound to be at the mercy of what has been handed to us through generational ties. Our obligation is to heal the past so the present is free for creative purpose. Loyalty, as we have been experiencing it, is most often to the past. A major component of war and prejudice involves invisible loyalties to family, race, nation, and religion. As we free the past, our loyalties are also freed. We can become loyal to ourselves and to creating a future that sustains life. There is wonder in the wisdom of older cultures that can put a concept as profound as the one expressed by Sankofa into just one word.

Six months into the diversity project it is time to test the premise that, given a safe space, given useful tools, and given a belief in the integrity of the human spirit, individuals would prefer to go beyond their comfort zones, would prefer to search for meaning, to go beyond antiquated patterns of personality that so often keep us in our positioned views of life. The hypothesis of the project stated that people joined together by economic necessity would increase productivity if given an opportunity to share their inner worlds, to dialogue in depth the issues they believe create a healthy, sustainable corporate culture. The hypothesis also stated that creative projects would come from within the group as a result of learning how to dialogue.

Dialogue comes from the Greek word *dialogos*. *Logos* means "the word" and *dia* means "through." An image presented by David Bohm about the nature of the dialogue is "a stream of meaning flowing among and through us and between us." This makes it possible to come to a shared understanding, to new creative ideas that may not have been there at the starting point.

Dialogue differs from discussion in a very basic way. Discussion means to break things up. It emphasizes the idea of analysis where there may be many points of view and where everybody presents a different one. In discussion you may agree with some points of view and disagree with others. In the end, it is a time to air our respective perspectives and find an alliance with those whose thinking matches ours. It is more like a game where there are winners and losers. Dialogue, on the other hand, has a different sort of spirit to it. It is more of a common participation in which we are playing a game with each other to make something more than we could do alone. Musical or dramatic improvisation is dialogue. Anyone who has ever been in a jam session or watched musicians permit the music to flow among and through and between them has a sense of the power and delight of dialogue. Having worked with the safety found in the dialogic model where desire was to find connections, the group was ready to tackle the next phase of diversity learning using the Sankofa Chart.

Nancy, a tall, thin, elegantly dressed woman stood nervously before a complex chart of circles and squares. Someone commented that it looked like a circuit board, a diagram of intricate electrical connections. That is perhaps an excellent description of the Sankofa Chart Nancy was about to present. The chart, also known as a genogram, has been used in the field of family therapy for decades. It is a shorthand process chart describing family and cultural influences of how we become who we are.

Nancy had been an observer for most of the past six months. She had been an upwardly mobile corporate executive ever since her graduation from a prestigious MBA program fifteen years earlier. She had learned to be politically correct, and it was rare

for her to speak out on controversial issues. She surprised everyone when she volunteered to be the first of the group to present
her family. She had asked for minimal help in preparing her
Sankofa Chart, yet is was obvious that she had spent a great deal
of time researching her family tree for this presentation. In
addition to the descriptive elements of the traditional genogram, the
Sankofa Chart, utilizing indigenous wisdom, requires the participants to consider the gifts as well as the challenges that have been
handed through the generations and to create action plans for the
conscious breaking of old self-defeating loyalty patterns.

The ancient cultures were highly conscious of the impact of
the past on the present. An Australian aborigine saying puts it
succinctly, "We carry our ancestors in our hearts, and sometimes
on our backs." Chief Seattle addresses generational responsibility
in his famous speech of 1851 when he responded to a proposed
treaty under which the Indians were persuaded to sell several
million acres of land around Puget Sound.

It begins,

> How can you buy or sell the sky, the
> warmth of the land? The idea is strange to
> us. If we do not own the freshness of the air
> and the sparkle of the water, how can you
> buy them...He [the white man] leaves his
> father's grave behind, and he does not care.
> He kidnaps the earth from his children, and
> he does not care. His father's grave, and his
> children's birthright are forgotten. He treats
> his mother, the earth, and his brother, the
> sky, as things to be bought, plundered, sold
> like sheep or bright beads. His appetite will
> devour the earth and leave behind only a
> desert.

And he challenges us.

> You must teach your children that the
> ground beneath their feet is the ashes of
> our grandfathers. So that they will respect
> the land, tell your children that the earth is
> rich with the lives of the kin. Teach your
> children what we have taught our children
> that the earth is our mother. Whatever
> befalls the earth befalls the sons of the

earth. If men spit upon the ground, they
spit upon themselves.

What is it we have been taught? What is it we are teaching
our children? Diversity training does, in fact, begin at home as the
Rodgers and Hammerstein lyrics from *South Pacific* show:

You've got to be taught to hate and fear
You've got to be taught from year to year
It's got to be drummed in your dear little ear
You've got to be carefully taught

You've got to be taught to be afraid
Of people whose eyes are oddly made
And people whose skin is a different shade
You've got to be carefully taught

You've got to be taught before it's too late
Before you are six or seven or eight
To hate all the people your relatives hate
You've got to be carefully taught

Our present culture has stagnated when considering generational responsibility and impact. In the past several decades,
we have become locked into the area of family dysfunction, of
what does not and has not worked. Coming from a dysfunctional
family has become an acceptable reason to abdicate self-respon-
sibility for personal life choices. Or, in the case of diversity, the
culture has received the limiting label of dysfunction. Mistrust,
polarization, discounting—all very real parts of our world—are
discussed over and over. It is much more of a rarity to consider
what is working. As a culture we are addicted to what is not
working. All one has to do is turn on the nightly news to prove this
point.

Utilizing the Sankofa Method for charting the personal and
societal ebb and flow of life, one is obligated to access the gifts (the
what-is-working aspects) and challenge (the what-is-to-be-over-
come aspects). In older cultures looking at one's life from this
broadened vantage point would be considered warrior work. In
today's vernacular we call it leadership training. Reframing one's
life is a call to action, an initiation. It is felt that before we can
redesign "out there," it is vital to put our own houses in order.

Doing one's own Sankofa Chart is part of the context of a
modern-day initiation. It can be used as an active, participatory
tool for personal growth. The more traditional use of the genogram
has been in the hands of family therapists as a diagnostic

indicator. The charts have the broader possibility of use as a resource for health beyond being an indicator of pathology. As we move from the information age to what we can hopefully call the age of empowerment, it is vital to teach individuals how to use effective personal growth tools rather than keep them solely in the hands of the mental health professional or seminar leader. Two examples of success in this area are the uses of the Myers-Briggs Type Indicator and the Enneagram, both gaining popularity as corporate growth tools.

Today is Nancy's initiation. It is no small thing to present one's family to a group of peers. There is nothing more personal, more sacred, more filled with primal energy and potential creativity than one's family history. This is no dry report filled merely with dates, it is the essence of who we have become, of how our personalities have taken shape, of how our hopes and dreams have manifested or fallen into stagnation, of how we have come to embrace or expel each other. Through our outer families, we have created our inner families, the ones we take with us for the rest of our lives even if we choose to never see our outer families again. Poet Juan Ramon Jimenez states the power of our inner memories in "A Remembrance Is Moving."

> A remembrance is moving
> down the long memory, disturbing
> the dry leaves with its delicate feet.
>
> Behind, the house is empty.
> On ahead, highways
> going on to other places, solitary highways,
> stretched out.
> And the rain is like weeping eyes,
> as if the eternal moment were going blind.
>
> Even though the house is quiet and shut,
> even though I am not in it, I am in it.
> And...good-bye, you who are walking
> without turning your head!

Nancy is ready, albeit filled with trepidation. She had volunteered to be "it," to be first. She stood, almost at attention, in front of her seventeen colleagues, each a manager of a different process area of a large corporation. Nancy chose to be first, she stated, because she was the representative from human resources. She felt human resources had shown limited vision in handling the diversity issue, and her concern was that there were already several equal opportunity lawsuits in house and many angry threats of more legal action from those who were feeling discounted. Two years of general diversity training for the entire corporation, she felt, had led nowhere. It had focused on demographics and profile charts and internal opinion poll results. It had been an academic exercise in complying with the laws of the land, all sound and fury, signifying nothing.

The general diversity training had stayed at the level of discussion rather than ever moving to dialogue. Initially the participants shared facts and then points of view. Often hypothetical work situations were presented, and people were asked to stand on one side of the room or the other, showing agreement or disagreement with what was presented. This merely continued the polarization. Once, a man ho had privately shared with Nancy the fact that he was a homosexual, went to "vote" by standing on the side of the room against health insurance for domestic partners so that no one would detect his secret. In the groups there were a few extremely vocal, highly opinionated individuals. The rest remained as silent as possible.

Nancy quoted from *Gentlemen's Agreement*, a bestselling book and Academy-Award winning film from the 1950s about anti-Semitism. "There is no more important work than beating down the complacency of essentially decent people about prejudice."

And so, not knowing where this exploration of her own life through the Sankofa process would take her and what it would mean to be witnessed by others, she was ready to plunge in. The group was curious and the room was filled with anticipation.

It is important to restate that the Sankofa Method has been developed to take people through a life skills process in incremental stages over a period of time. This program is not meant for a pep rally type day- or week-long seminar. It is meant for companies that really want to work through problems at a systems level rather than at a symptoms level. One year has been designated the appropriate amount of time. When working at a depth level, periods of integration are needed to practice and strengthen the skills that are taught. Individuals are prepared for this process with an awareness that we are dealing with the basic building blocks of life, with raw energy that is filled with pitfalls if the container is not safe. One only has to think about the play *Who's Afraid of Virginia Wolfe* to see what happens when our defenses are removed in a dinner party type environment. Day or week programs without follow-up become like a meal of desserts, one is comfortable for a while and vitally hungry and unsatiated soon after.

Nancy had spent six months in preparation for today. And so, with a deep breath she invited her colleagues to meet, through narrative, her parents, her siblings, her world. Nancy took us back four generations to roots in a small South Carolina town when the Civil War was ending.

Nancy was one of the three African American managers in the group. We sat in a room we could almost call "Little America," a microcosm of the macrocosm. Much of the diversity was obvious. Black, White, Asian, Chicano, female, male were easily defined. Religion and nationality, less obvious, had often come to the fore over the months. People were willing to talk about being Catholic or Baptist or Irish or Greek. There was a comfort level regarding these issues that would have been more awkward in past decades. These areas had been acknowledged as foundations upon which we could build.

Seeing some progress in human relationships from past decades was a relief. It gave hope that the concerns of the present would become faded memories for future generations. Racism and feminism were "hot" issues. Homosexuality was a quiet question mark, and economic diversity had not yet been touched. The room was filled with the human dilemma, with what we have already created, with the subtle desire to hopefully grow beyond, and with the fear of leaving the familiar.

Nancy's narrative was, in many respects, everyone's story. It was a story of unlimited hopes and relinquished dreams, of hugs and hurts and betrayals and courage. The actors in Nancy's personal play were uniquely hers, the themes universal. Nancy related a story her mother had shared recently. It was a story sprinkled with laughter, tinged with bitterness, and laced with sadness. Nancy had to "go home again" to gather information for her Sankofa Chart. She admitted surprise at how much personal healing had taken place on the way to complete the graph that she pointed to now. Nancy had harbored deep resentment toward her mother for all the yelling and arguing she had experienced as a youngster. She had grown into a quiet and reserved woman, who rarely spoke up and felt that any type of arguing was crude. She had remained an aloof grown daughter, and any talk at family gatherings remained superficial chitchat. She refrained from being alone with her mother as much as possible.

Her mother, now in her mid-seventies, had been suspicious when Nancy first came to visit. There was no cautious chit-chat now. Nancy began gently asking questions about long-buried hurts. Nancy had learned to ask dialogue-enhancing questions that had the possibility for opening to deeper relationships. Questions would begin with "I wonder" or "I'm curious." These simple words help to open doors to the deeper talk. Nancy knew much about how her mother had handled being a grown-up in a large city on the East Coast. She had judged her mother and never let go of her deep resentment. She was glad she had sons and didn't have to carry the empty mother-daughter relationship forward. But now a change was taking place. She wondered aloud with her mother what it was like to be a little girl in a rural town in the South, way before Rosa Parks ever sat in the front of that bus.

Nancy's mother responded to her daughter's honest curiosity and opened the gates to a childhood that had been padlocked long ago. She shared with her daughter the shame of the fun-loving seven-year-old who had to walk several miles to the black school, right past the white school where the kids would shout "nigger" and throw orange peels. The seven-year-old's shame was raw, the ancient hurt real when Nancy's mother said, "I never could get why color mattered more than character. And ever since then I became a fighter. I swore I'd never let anyone see me cry. And I've never cried another tear from that day." Nancy, barely audible, reported to the diversity group that at that moment she saw her mother for the first time, not the angry women she detested but the little girl whose blackness made her vow to be feisty and hide soft feelings. She permitted the group to share the tender moments of rectification that occurred when Nancy had put her hand on her mother's arm. Grown daughter and aging mother let the sweet taste of the salty tears heal the years of distance.

In doing her Sankofa Chart, Nancy had grown stronger. She had learned that honoring diversity begins at home. That she could not judge or condemn anyone for not facing the Black-White issue or any other diversity issue when she had not faced her own deep prejudice against her own mother for not being the way she wanted her to be. She saw the roots of prejudice from a wider perspective.

Over the intervening months, her relationships at home blossomed and her job responsibilities increased. She had renewed zeal for life, and she took time to engage in her own self-nurturing. She and her mother would go to lunch and laugh and learn about each other. She smiled in her gentle, reserved manner as she said to the group, "I now know what rectification work feels like inside me. It has not only changed my relationship with my mom, but it has also taken the taboo from arguing and has helped me be able to be more present when unpleasant things happen both at work and at home. My husband and sons say I'm not as tough to be around when they want to handle disagreements in a noisy manner."

However, Nancy had one area of deep concern. She reported back to the group that some of her African American friends in the corporation became angry with her for no longer agreeing with their more militant views. They were determined to bring the corporation to its knees through long, drawn-out legal battles—as many as possible. They had waited long enough for change to occur, and they would fight the battle. Nancy was seen as a turncoat, and they began to shun her, leaving her out of lunch discussions and weekend parties. It was the first time she had ever experienced prejudice from her own people. There were periods of doubt and she thought about withdrawing from the diversity program rather than lose her important friendships. Her mother, at one of their frequent luncheons, suggested she share her upset with "those diversity people."

"They helped us find a way to come together," Nancy's mother mused. "Isn't that what diversity is all about, coming together and still being yourself?"

New forms of relating were beginning among the eighteen diversity participants. Diversity took on a deeper meaning, the us versus them attitude at the onset of the program had given way to "we're all in it together," and creative options began to flow in the group dialogues.

The months continued and each manager was given the opportunity to come forward and present his or her family. Initially only a few had volunteered. Doing one's Sankofa Chart had been a suggestion, not a mandate. There was no requirement to stand in front of the room and present such sacred life material. Yet, eventually, everyone requested a day and the program was lengthened until each manager had his or her turn. The request came from within the group and was one of the many pleasant surprises for the facilitators.

The wisdom of indigenous teachings states that once someone is witnessed in an initiation he or she cannot easily go back to the old patterns and behaviors, and once someone has been a witness to another's initiation he or she is changed forever. That certainly was the case in this diversity training program. Changes were evident both in the workplace and at home.

Each presentation built on the one before. The tapestry of human explorations enriched the group. Wounds about color and gender and race were given the healing salve of deep listening, and the long process of real healing began. The group had committed to the sacred privilege of truth telling in the sessions and an agreement had been made to maintain silence about content outside of the group. A new understanding of boundaries was explored. An older model of boundaries, especially in the corporate world, revolved around staying silent and covering your rear. This newer model states the truth will set you free and you are responsible for the time and place of your communications. Personal responsibility is a key to rightful leadership. Leaders are obligated to speak out and a key to responsible leadership considers the where and the how as much as the what and the why.

As the uniqueness of each individual was celebrated, there was a release of pent-up individual energy that gave way to both personal and collective creativity. Everyone had chosen to make the journey homeward to do the rectification work necessary to be fully present.

The managers reported that their listening skills had changed dramatically. They began to hear the subtle language of fear as the driving force beneath the racial jokes and sexual innuendoes. They began to see everyday life from a both/and rather than an either/or perspective. The duality of life slowly gave way to a vision of connectedness. They looked at each person as both an adult in the workplace and as someone's child, which helped them see the whole person more clearly. They used words like "I wonder" and "I'm curious" to open conversations. They permitted themselves freedom for dialogue to develop. They found them-selves slowing the pace of conversation rather than rushing to the comfort of quick solutions, an admitted unhandled addiction in the business world. Paradoxically, they got more creative work done through the less structured and agenda-driven dialogue model than through linear problem-solving methods.

Nancy, as she grew stronger in her capacity to view life from a systems perspective, went to her African American colleagues to offer another perspective, another paradigm. She talked with them about her newly emerging belief in the connectedness of life and how they could find new ways to be heard beyond the win-lose legal system. Initially suspicious, they listened in a polite, neutral manner. Over a period of time, she once again became a sought-after luncheon companion. Eventually, several lawsuits were dropped and a committee was formed to consider creative ways for minority input concerning issues of hiring and promotion. Senior management, impressed with the willingness to find a better way, offered to send representatives to participate in monthly progress meetings. Nancy felt the courage she had gained in going to talk with her mother kept her strong as she began the new conversations with her peers and with senior management. She joined a team to write a paper on how rebalancing personal relationship lines and freeing invisible loyalties to family patterns are deterrents to prejudice and positionality in the workplace.

As the workplace becomes more diverse, consciousness has to be raised to examine policies and practices that do not foster cooperation and creativity. It becomes vital for companies to look at their policies for attracting and maintaining business. Many companies wait until they have litigation and are in a reactive, polarized place. Others are beginning to consider a preventive model to be as productive as possible in order to compete in the global marketplace.

The combination of dialogue, family rectification work and reclamation of the wisdom of the indigenous peoples forms an exciting model. It is helpful to use demographics and academic studies that are the cornerstone of many present-day diversity programs. It is then important to build a more personally-tailored program. The business of business beyond the bottom line is to help employees grow and handle conflicts responsibly.

In an atmosphere of open-heartedness it is very difficult to permit the prejudices we have inherited from past generations and past cultural times to determine our future course. Witnessing and being witnessed as we put our lives in our own chosen order is a major initiation needed in a time when we have permitted rituals and initiations of personal strength to be cast aside. We no longer live in a time, where to become a warrior, we must slay a lion. We live in a time where warriors are known as leaders, and as leaders we must learn to tame the lion. Nothing has a more frightening or powerful roar than the legacies and loyalties coming from our past generations.

BJ Gallagher Hateley is an accomplished management consultant, speaker, author, and filmmaker. Her clients include DaimlerChrysler, Southern California Edison, IBM, Chevron, John Deere Credit and Phoenix Newspapers Inc., among others.

She spent nearly five years as Manager of Training and Development for *The Los Angeles Times* and, prior to that, she was the Director of Staff Training and Professional Development for the University of Southern California. She has published articles in *The L.A. Times*, *Training* magazine, and *Training and Development Journal*, among others.

Warren H. Schmidt, PhD, a Professor Emeritus of the University of Southern California and UCLA, is president of Chrysalis, Inc., a management training and consulting company. He is the co-author, with Jerry Finnegan, of *The Race Without a Finish Line: America's Quest for Total Quality*, as well as *TQManager*.

Hateley and Schmidt are the co-authors of *A Peacock in the Land of Penguins: A Tale of Diversity and Discovery*.

15

Ruffled Feathers in the Land of Penguins

BJ Gallagher Hateley & Warren H. Schmidt

Illustrations by Sam Weiss

The penguins were in trouble and they knew it.

For many years they had ruled the Land of Penguins
    with unquestioned authority.
They had built a great enterprise that grew and thrived
    in the Sea of Organizations.
Penguins were seen as models of success.
And for a long time their world was orderly and predictable.

But there came a time when things began to change
    in the Land of Penguins.
No one really noticed at first
    that a few new birds had begun living in their Land —
        birds who were exotic and different in many ways.

No one paid much attention to them —
>   after all, there were just a few of them,
>   and they lived on low-level perches,
>   not bothering anyone.
>They did their work and seemed content.
>They knew their place in the pecking order,
>   so everyone was comfortable and secure.

But over time, more and more of these new birds
>   appeared in the Land of Penguins.

"Where are all these strange birds coming from?"
>   the penguins asked themselves.
>They were beginning to feel uneasy.
>   "These new birds don't understand how we do things here."
>   "They don't fit in. They have strange habits."
>   "How can they ever hope to be successful here?"

A few of the penguins were more optimistic
>   in their assessment of the situation.
>   "Actually, it's good to have these exotic birds here."
>   "They work hard and have good ideas."
>   "Maybe we should be trying to bring in even *more* new
>   birds, to make up for keeping them out in the past."

The issue of the exotic birds became a regular topic
>   of discussion and debate among the penguins.

As the years went by, the situation worsened.
  Tensions between the new birds and the penguins escalated.
  Tensions between groups of the exotic birds
    also became apparent.
  As tension mounted, conflict increased —
    and productivity decreased.

More and more time and energy was diverted
    into handling grievances and complaints.
  The exotic birds had worked hard
    to prove themselves to the penguins,
    and they wanted to be recognized and promoted.
  The younger penguins were frustrated
    because they, too, had worked hard,
    and feared that the exotic birds
    threatened their chances for success.

Morale became a serious problem —
  Some of the exotic birds left for other lands,
    and so did some of the junior penguins,
  deciding that their futures were too limited
    in the Land of Penguins.

"What to do? What to do?" the penguins asked themselves.
  They knew they were in a tough spot.
  If they did nothing, the situation in their Land
    would undoubtedly deteriorate.
  This was so unlike anything they had ever experienced before.
  They could see no clear or obvious solution to their troubles.

One day, a couple of the VIPs (Very Important Penguins) discussed the problem over lunch.

"You know, this situation with the exotic birds is really troubling," said one of them.

"I agree," replied the other, "and it's taking a heavy toll on our Land."

"Maybe we're too close to the situation. Maybe what we need is to get some distance, so that we can look at the issue more objectively and see what to do."

"What are you suggesting?"

"Well, when I have a puzzling problem, I like to swim out to an iceberg where I can be alone and take some time to sort things out. Getting some distance and having some solitude helps me look at problems from a broader perspective."

"Do you think the same thing would work if several of us went out to an iceberg? I know it works for you as an individual, but will it work for a group?"

"I don't know, but it sure seems like it's worth a try. We're not getting anywhere trying to sort things out here in the Land of Penguins. Maybe we could see the situation more clearly if we weren't right in the middle of it."

"I agree. Let's see if the other VIPs will join us."

And so it came to pass that the Very Important Penguins set aside a day to swim out to "Iceberg Incommunicado" for an executive retreat to try to resolve their troubles with the exotic birds.

As they settled themselves into comfortable positions on the iceberg, an air of expectancy was apparent.
    They knew that important issues were at hand.
    The future of their Land was on the line.
No one knew what the outcome would be,
    but they all knew that the stakes were high.

President Peter Penguin cleared his throat,
signaling that the meeting was about to begin.
    "I want to thank you all for taking time
        from your busy schedules to be here today,"
            he intoned in his deep, resonant voice.
    "Things are changing in the Sea of Organizations,
        and we face many challenges that are totally new to us.
    Ironically, one of the most critical challenges is not *outside*
        but rather *inside* our Land.
        Our biggest threat right now stems from all the various
        exotic birds who live there.
    I don't need to tell any of you how important this issue is.
        We've all seen what's been happening in recent years,
        and we all share the frustration and concern.
    We have to develop a strategy, a plan.
    Just letting things evolve, I'm afraid, is going to lead to disaster.
    The time has come for us to really grapple with this issue —
        to look deep into ourselves and into our organization to
        see what kind of a future we're going to create for
            ourselves.
    Nothing less than the future of the Land of Penguins rests with
        us here today!"
President Peter Penguin sat down decisively and looked expectantly
    around the group.
        "Who'd like to begin the discussion?"

There were a few moments of silence
   as each penguin thought about what he wanted to say.

Finally, Patrick Penguin, the VIP of Planning, broke the silence.
   "Well, several things seem clear to me —
   First: The exotic birds are here to stay. They're a fact of
         life here in our Land, and we have to deal with that.
   Second: We're still in charge. This is *our* Land — that's the
      way it's always been, and that's the way it should stay.
   Third: Our record of success speaks for itself. We had a long
      illustrious history before the exotic birds came in —
      we clearly know what it takes to be successful.
   Fourth: Our mistake has been in letting these birds have
      too much influence on the organization. We've let them
      disrupt us, and the result has been *more* conflict, *more*
      problems, and *less* productivity.
   It's time to reassert control over our own Land. It's time to
      show them who's the boss. We call the shots. We need to
      take charge and put all those other birds back in their
      places. They can stay and play a part in the future of the
      Land of Penguins — but we have to stay in charge. We
      can use their energy and their talent, but we must not to
      give away our power or control.
   I also think it's important that we closely monitor and
      control how many and what kinds of exotic birds we let in
      here in the future. You know, they have different habits,
      different lifestyles, and they sing different songs. When
      you get too many differences, it just tears the place apart.
   So I'm advocating a **Strategy of Command and Control**."

With that, Patrick Penguin plunked himself down on his seat.

"Any comments?" queried President Peter Penguin.

"I'd like to comment," responded Palmer Penguin, the VIP in
charge of Penguin Personnel.

 "I certainly can understand Patrick's position, and I appreciate
 his concerns about control versus chaos. I have a great
 deal of respect for Patrick and the contributions he's
 made to our Land.

 But the thought occurs to me that perhaps the past is not our
 best guide for how to deal with the future.

 'Control' has been the watchword of the past, but I think the
 future is going to look very different.

 Perhaps we need a new paradigm of how to operate.

 Maybe instead of 'control,' we should emphasize 'cooperation,'
 or 'collaboration.'

"Let me elaborate a bit...

 All of us here today are penguins. We are great at teamwork;
 we share common values; we all have a similar
 perspective. We have our feet planted firmly on the
 ground (or the ice, as the case may be!).

 We are also excellent swimmers, and we have been very
 successful in getting all the fish we need to survive.

 But there are some things we *cannot* do —

 like fly, or run fast, or make nests in high places.

 Many of our exotic birds *can* do these things.

 Some can soar through the sky and see great distances.
 (Have you watched Edward the Eagle lately?)

 Others have powerful legs that can propel them at amazing
 speeds and give them a powerful kick.
 (I am thinking of Ozzie the Ostrich.)

 And still others can build nests in high places and protect the
 future of their species. (Mildred the Mud-dauber makes
 particularly creative nests.)"

"It seems to me that we could learn a lot from these birds —
    things that could be very important to our future.
  I know we've been successful in the past, as Patrick so clearly
    pointed out,
        but I don't think we should rely on that forever.

"The Sea of Organizations has been getting more and more turbulent.
  The storms are more frequent,
      the waves are stronger,
        and the wind is more powerful.
The climate around us is changing in many ways.
In the Sea of Organizations, we are seeing new currents
  moving in swiftly from the distant east,
  and unusual patterns shifting in
    what we thought was the predictable west.

"I think we should be tapping into the 'differentness' of our exotic
  birds, and embracing it is an asset to be shared,
      rather than as a disruptive influence to be controlled.
We need to welcome these exotic birds as our partners —
  sharing information, power, and rewards.
We stand to benefit far more from working *collaboratively with
  them* rather than trying to *control* them.
I urge that we adopt a **Strategy of Productive Partnership**."

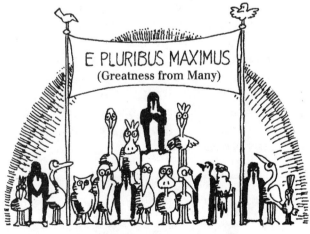

The group was impressed
  with Palmer Penguin's articulate persuasiveness.
There was silence as they reflected on
  the vision he had outlined for their future.

But Paul Penguin, the VIP in charge of Production,
     seemed visibly upset. He had shifted restlessly in his seat
     while Palmer was making his remarks,
     and he shook his head frequently, frowning his disagreement.
No longer able to contain his feelings, he jumped to his feet.

"I gotta tell ya, all this talk just ticks me off! The situation seems
          very clear to me. We never shoulda let those birds in
          here in the first place.
     I said it before and I'll say it again —
          the Land of Penguins is a place for *penguins*,
               not other types of birds.
          They've got no business in our Land.
     They can't cut it; they don't fit in;
          all they do is cause problems;
               and now the whole place is a mess!
"They expect us to change *our* ways
     so that *they* will 'feel more comfortable.'
     What's this 'comfortable' crap?
     Nobody ever talked like that when *I* was a young bird.
     You worked hard, paid your dues, didn't complain,
          and if you were good enough, you made it to the top.
               That's how I made it to where I am today.
     It's a good system, it's simple, and that's how it oughta be.
     If those new birds can't adapt, they should leave.
          It's as simple as that.
All this 'understanding' and 'partnership' stuff
     you guys are talking about is just a bunch of guano!
We don't need a *new* strategy — we need the *old* one —
     a return to the **Strategy of the Good Ol' Days!**"

And with that, he turned and stomped away from the group.

The VIPs were stunned by the vehemence of Paul's outburst.
Everyone had known for a long time
   that he was against letting the new birds in,
   but they were surprised that he'd be so open about his
   hostility in front of his boss and the other VIPs.
Some secretly agreed with Paul's position,
   but they hesitated to say so publicly,
     for fear of being "politically incorrect"
     or being seen as a bird-bigot.

President Peter Penguin tried to defuse the tension in the air.
   "Maybe we should take a short break
     and come back and resume our discussion.
   Why don't we all stand up, stretch our wings and legs a bit,
     and have some refreshments —
     herring and cod are being served over by the water.
   We'll reconvene in half an hour."

The group was visibly relieved to have a break.

No one was quite sure what to do or how to respond to Paul.
They all respected him for the long service
   he'd given to the Land of Penguins.
He had been a mentor to several of them,
   and they felt a great deal of loyalty and gratitude to him.
But at the same time, many suspected that some of Paul's thinking —
   while appropriate for an earlier time in their history —
     might now be outdated.

As the Very Important Penguins strolled around the iceberg,
   they talked quietly among themselves,
     comparing notes on what had been said
       and speculating on where this might all end up.
It seemed that their VIP retreat was turning out
   to be as tension filled as life in their Land.

Everyone was eager to find a resolution
   to the problem of the exotic birds,
     but they seemed no closer to a solution
     than when they had started.
The problem seemed to be getting more confused
   the more they talked about it.

When the group sat down together again,
    Paul Penguin was back in their midst.
    He had obviously calmed down,
        but the cool, distant look on his face
        told the others that his position had not changed.

President Peter Penguin cleared his throat again.
    "Shall we continue?"

"I'd be interested in hearing what *you* think,"
    Palmer Penguin suggested, looking at the president.
"Surely you have some opinions on this."

"Yes, I do," replied Peter Penguin.
    "But as President, I don't want to unduly influence
        the discussion by expressing my views right now.
    I'd rather wait until you all have shared your perspectives."

"That makes sense," Palmer agreed.
    "Well then, who's got some other ideas to share?"

"I have a suggestion," responded Penny Penguin, the VIP of
Public Relations.
   "Why don't we put all the exotic birds
       through a special training program?
   It seems to me that the problem is
       that they don't know how to behave properly
           and what it takes to be successful in our Land.
   But nobody has ever really taken the time to train them,
       coach them, and incorporate them into our culture.
   We can encourage them all to wear penguin suits,
       and we can train them to shorten their stride —
           to walk the penguin walk —
               and talk the penguin talk.
   We could even set up a special high-potential program,
       giving them a fast track development plan.
   We could put some of them on task force projects
               where they'd learn a lot and get good visibility.
   And the birds who weren't in this program would get the
       message very quickly about what it takes to 'make it' in
       the Land of Penguins.
   I'd like to think of it as
       the **Strategy of Developing Penguin Potential**.

"What do you all think?"
   She looked around at the other VIP faces
       to assess their level of agreement.

"Well, that's one idea,
    but I have another approach that I'd like to put on the table —
        one that I think is even *better* than that,"
    asserted Putney Penguin,
        as he brushed past Penny
            to step into the center of the group.

Putney was the VIP of Product Development,
    and he had something of a reputation
        for coming up with ideas that were very creative —
    but sometimes "off-the-wall" from the others' point of view.
He was pretty flashy as penguins go,
    always impeccably groomed,
        in a penguin suit with very stylish lines.
He loved to admire himself
    as he caught his reflection in the ice.
Everyone knew he had a big ego,
    but he had been responsible for some major breakthroughs
        in the Land of Penguins,
            so his flamboyant style was shrugged off with,
                "Oh well, that's just Putney."

His voice escalated as he paced excitedly around the center of
the group:
"Now picture this...
We reorganize the Land of Penguins into different divisions.
In the Headquarters division we'll have 'Penguin Enterprises,'
   carrying on all the activities
      that have made us so successful.
Only penguins will work there, of course,
   so things should go ultra-smoothly.
Then we'll take these exotic birds
   and set up separate divisions for them —
      they will each specialize in what they know and do best.
We'll have a division for birds who sing,
   one for birds who hunt,
      one for birds who build great nests,
         and so on.
A penguin will be the Director of each of these divisions,
   of course, and he'll have a specialist bird as his assistant.
Whaddya think so far?
And I think *I'd* be the *perfect* VIP
   to head up those special divisions —
      I've got good rapport with a lot of those birds
   and I think I could really leverage their creativity
      into some promising new ventures.
Isn't this a great idea? Don'tcha just love it?
We could call it the **Strategy of Potential New Products!**"

Putney was bubbling with enthusiasm
      by the time he finished his pitch.

Patrick and Paul exchanged knowing glances
    as they shook their heads.

"Yeah, right, Putney," Patrick interjected.
    "This sounds like another one of your wild schemes.
    Remember the time you brought in
        that slick, fast-talking gooney bird consultant
            who was going to teach us all to fly?
    What a disaster that was!
    Screeching and squawking,
        feathers flying,
            broken bones —
                Geez!
    Have you been listening to some consultant again?
    Or did you come up with this idea all on your own?"

Paul chuckled his agreement as he lit up a seaweed cigar.
    "I agree with Patrick.
    Sounds to me like some pie-in-the-sky fantasy
        that will never get off the ground —
            or if it does, it'll soon crash."

The whole group chuckled nervously as they remembered
    their embarrassment over the flying escapade.

President Peter jumped into the conversation.
    "Now, let's not get personal here. I'm sure we've all been
    associated with projects or ideas in the past that we'd just
    as soon forget.
        We don't need to dredge up old issues.
        We're in an exploratory mode here,
            considering all our options,
                so let's keep an open mind.
    Now, is there anyone we haven't heard from yet?
    How about you, Percy Penguin?
    You've been very quiet throughout this discussion.
    You're the VIP in charge of Purchasing, and you've got a lot
        of these exotic birds working for you —
            what do you think?"

Percy was one of the most thoughtful members
    of the penguin establishment,
        generally regarded as a solid citizen.
He was usually quiet,
    but when he did speak,
        his comments were always worthwhile.
He thought for a moment.

"Well," he said, "I've been giving this a lot of thought
    as I've been listening to the rest of you,
    and I must say that I've been surprised and puzzled
    by some of the comments I've heard here.
Personally, I've had really good experiences
    with these new birds.
Sure, they sound different from us,
    and maybe they go about their work
        in a different way than I would.
But they seem to accomplish what needs to be done —
    at least the exotic birds who work for me do.
I guess I've been kind of quiet through this whole debate
    because I don't see much of a problem.
Things have been going pretty well
    in my part of the Land of Penguins.
It's hard for me to come up with a solution if I don't have a
    problem," he shrugged.

Patrick Penguin looked skeptical.
"How come we're all having problems with these new birds
    and you're not? Are you really leveling with us?"

The other VIPs were puzzled too.
Was Percy just trying to look good in front of the group?

Penny Penguin chimed in,
"I've never known Percy to be anything less
    than totally honest.
Maybe he just sees something that the rest of us don't."

Percy smiled,
"Actually, Penny, that's close,
    but I'd say it a little differently
It's more like, I don't see something that the rest of you see.
You all view the new birds as a 'problem,' and I don't.
You might say that my strategy is
    the **Strategy That There IS No Problem**,
        and I manage my birds accordingly."

Palmer from Personnel looked again at President Peter Penguin.
  "We still haven't heard what *you* think, sir.
    We don't seem to have any agreement here —
      maybe you have the solution."

"Yes, what do you think, chief?"
  asked the Very Important Penguins.

They were frustrated by the lack of progress
    in their executive retreat
  and hoped that their leader
    would have the definitive solution for them.

President Peter looked around
 at all the expectant faces of his VIP team.
Then he leaned back,
 glanced thoughtfully up at the sky,
  and slowly began to speak:
 "You know, I came here today with great hopes
  that we would come up with a solution to our problem
   of what to do about the exotic birds.
 It is clear that you've all given this a lot of thought,
  and I know you care deeply about the future well-being
   of the Land of Penguins.
 Your proposed solutions reflect your personal experiences
  and how you think an organization should function.
 But it seems that we are no closer to a solution
  than when we started this morning.
 We are deeply divided
  and don't seem to have much common ground,
   except that we all are concerned
    about the future of our Land.
 I find myself wondering...
  What's missing in our discussion?
  Have we overlooked something — or someONE?
  Should we have invited some of the exotic birds here
   to tell us about *their* perspectives and ideas?
  Or would we just be raising expectations we cannot meet?
 I don't know. I have to admit that I am really stumped."

He paused with a deep sigh,
 the weight of it all heavy on his mind.

Then in a quiet voice he concluded —

 "Now, if only we were HUMANS,
  we would know EXACTLY what to do,
   wouldn't we?"

THE END

Joy Carver is president of Joy Carver and Associates, which offers clients over 25 years of experience in general management, education, and training in public and private sector organizations. As an organizational development consultant, she helps clients compete in the domestic and international marketplace by enabling them to move beyond perceived barriers and to expand their vision of the future.

Clients include AT&T; Showboat Casino; Coca-Cola; Taylor Made; Honeywell; Delaware Health and Social Services; and Xerox.

Before establishing her own company, she was a performance consultant with Pecos River Learning Center, where she designed and delivered performance improvement programs for employees at all levels. As director of executive management development for Honeywell, Inc., Carver managed the formulation and implementation of company-wide training and developmental policies and strategies that supported corporate operating priorities.

16

A Matter of Respect

Joy Carver

"We teach best, what we need to learn most."

If only I would stop my internal chatter long enough, long enough to *listen* to your cries. Your cries to be heard, to be understood, to be listened to, to be respected...with all my sight, with all my hearing, with all my *heart*, and with *all my soul.* Maybe, just maybe, we could dance in conversation and

- support one another's vision
- support one another's right to be
- coordinate effective action together
- understand, value, and celebrate our rich variety

What would it truly be like? What would it take?

* * * * *

This is a story about two well-intentioned people who failed miserably to utilize their skills in listening, self-observation, and self-correction. They found themselves in a fruitless discussion trying to get "their point" across at all costs. When they reached the point of diminishing returns, they agreed to stop the discussion and continue it at a later date.

Joy's Perspective

It was around 9:30 P.M. on Thursday night when I arrived at the Philadelphia International Airport. I had been driving for four hours after having facilitated a three-day intensive workshop. My mind was very much on the presentation that Robert and I planned to produce for a major client.

> *[This is an example of the different ways we listen. We each hear something different. We each attach our own weight to the story—the words being said and the emotions we feel.]*

The Conversation

Joy: Hi, Robert, I just arrived at the airport and I'm exhausted. I still need to catch a plane and get a bite to eat. I promised to call you and share some of my thinking about next week's design. I have a great idea to share with you. [I shared my vision for the session.]

Robert: Joy, I've been working on a design, and I faxed it to you. Oh, you probably haven't gotten it yet because you haven't been home. Tell me why you sent such a long list of objectives for our session to the client. Does she expect us to cover all of those topics in an hour and a half? I would really have liked to have seen it before you sent it to her.

> *[During this conversation, both of us were engaged in a ping-pong match, attempting to be heard without listening to the other. Notice that we are talking about two different issues, the design of the upcoming presentation and what was sent to our client.]*

Robert: Well, you said you would and then you didn't. I left you a couple of messages and did not get a response back from you.

Joy: I got your messages Saturday afternoon. Your last message said that you were leaving for New York about 4:00 so I waited until later to phone you and leave a message. I did the best I could under the circumstances. [I cannot recall what Robert said next until I heard him say the words, "I don't feel respected."] I felt attacked and threatened and threw back to him, "Robert, I wouldn't be going through this if Mel were working with me."

Robert: What do you mean?

* * * * *

We both realized the conversation wasn't going anywhere. We agreed to talk again in a couple of days. It was during that time of reflection that we decided to reenact our communication breakdown as our presentation. Our focus was respect, and I felt this would be an excellent experience to share, especially since we had not reached a resolution.

Now, before I go any further, wouldn't you like to hear Robert's recap of the same situation?

Robert's Perspective

I waited all week to speak to Joy. I was keyed up about our upcoming program, which was fast approaching. Very much on my mind were some open issues with Joy that had been bothering me. Speaking to Joy always seemed to require adjusting to her schedule and now, given the upcoming call, I was anxious to resolve our issues.

The Conversation

Joy: Hi, Robert, I'm at the airport. I'm exhausted. I just finished my work in Maryland, I've been on the road for four hours, I still have to catch a flight, and I barely have time to eat. But I said I'd call and I came up with some great ideas for our program on the way up. [Joy shared her ideas that I was confused by.] So what do you think?

Robert: [Pause] I guess I like the idea of getting in deeper. I wrote an outline myself. Let me share what I did. [I quickly presented my ideas and felt that I wasn't connecting with Joy at all.] That outline you sent to the client—did you mean that we were actually going to do all that in an hour and a half?

Joy: No, those were just some ideas. I wanted to show her the things we could do.

Robert: Oh, I get it. It was long and I didn't see how we could do it in the time we had. You know, you said you'd call to go over the outline with me. Then you didn't call Saturday morning as you promised, and I left you three messages.

Joy: But I did call.

Robert: Yes, but on Sunday [Joy remembers leaving the message on Saturday] and after you had already faxed the outline.

Joy: Robert, I had *no time.* I did the best I could. If I had had time, I would have sent it. They called me late Friday night. I called you immediately and I did what I could. I had to get it out right away. You should be grateful I did it.

Robert: Yes, OK, but at least if you had given me some context, that these were only some ideas. You could have written that on the fax...I thought we should be in alignment. [I didn't feel included.] The bottom line is that I didn't feel respected.

Joy: [Beginning to cry] I'm on fumes right now. If you were Mel or Sandra, I wouldn't even be having this conversation. I'm giving you this work and I could be doing it all myself. But I'll still honor my agreement to do this project with you.

Robert: Joy, look, I care for you very much. This isn't working. Why don't we talk some other time. We're not going to work this out right now.

* * * * *

Robert and I began to ask ourselves about the situation we have described to you from our individual recollections.

- How did this situation occur?
- What were the conditions that supported this communication breakdown?
- Where could we look to better understand how we co-created this experience?
- What could be learned from this experience and then shared with others?

Robert and I concluded that we could look to a previous learning experience we had in common. It was a course called Ontological Design...the study of your life, which was presented by Dr. Fernando Flores. It provided us with an opportunity to explore what it is to be human. From Dr. Flores as well as two other pioneers in ontological coaching, Dr. Rafael Echeverria and Julio Ollala, we learned how the three domains—biology, history, and language—could help us understand how we listen and respond to one another.

The Heart of the Matter

We have found the three domains of biology, history, and language extremely helpful for understanding how we listen and respond to one another. While we cannot prevent every negative or uncomfortable breakdown from happening, we can resolve to learn from our interactions, identify alternative actions, and approach future situations with more insight.

The first domain is that of biology. We are in a continual state of adaptation, seeking to ensure our safety and survival. This drive, triggered by our ongoing interactions with our environment, operates in virtually everything we do. Who we see as threats and as opportunities may be less a matter of deliberate choice and more a matter of reflexive habit formed out of our inherent concern for protection and safety. Racism, despicable as it is, could be partially understood as a matter of behavior patterns acquired long ago that at one time helped protect us from the real or imagined danger of those viewed as different from ourselves. And perhaps out of our fears of one another, certain groups of people chose to oppress others lest they be oppressed or suffer a loss of control.

Concerns for "survival" (safety and security needs around money issues and timelines for their joint commitments) kicked into Robert's situation while Joy's concerns were of basic physical needs, such as food and sleep, and to keep her promise to call Robert.

Robert felt threatened that he would not be able to continue with the project for the client, or perhaps on any project, with Joy in the future. Unconsciously, Joy shifted her concern from her basic needs to safety and security needs by responding defensively when Robert said that he didn't feel respected.

Robert noticed that his body was tense and he was upset with Joy, but he pulled back, not wanting to inflame her since he knew she was stressed. Joy noticed that her body was tense and felt that she was being attacked, criticized, and blamed for situations that were not in her control. She had shared her physical condition with Robert up front and also felt a lack of respect given the lateness of the hour.

By becoming keener observers of our own and other's automatic instinct for protection and survival, we can observe and modify our biological states. We can intervene on our own behalf by checking our breathing, noticing where tension is experienced in our bodies, listing to the tone of our voices, observing our body language and posture, and facial expressions.

Our bodies send signals that affect others around us, much as what occurs between animals in the wild. To intervene in our situation, Robert took some calming, deep breaths when Joy began to cry. Though still anxious, he became centered enough to propose that they speak at another time. Robert reports that Joy became less threatening to him and he was able to move on as a result. Joy's crying was a big release of stress for her since she was triggered by her perceived demands from Robert. She told Robert that she couldn't continue the conversation at that point and was able to move on as well.

Learning goes way beyond having information, developing the "right techniques," and following a prescription—it involves our whole bodies, including our hearts and minds. Learning is a process of training our neuromuscular systems to develop new awareness and practices. We can consciously choose to adapt ourselves to an environment that will not always feel safe or familiar to us. This requires great flexibility, courage, and consideration.

History, the second domain, also has great power in shaping how we interact with one another. It encompasses our personal and group memory that is reflected in our traditions, practices, standards, and differing values and beliefs. History, like biology, is often unobserved. Much of it is interpretation of the past and is revealed to us in beliefs about what is right, wrong, good, bad, possible, or impossible. While Robert's breakdown occurred in the present, his communication breakdown was also about some past issues where he hadn't reached resolution with Joy and had experienced a sense of powerlessness. Joy was operating in the present, but with little fuel to sustain the level of intensity Robert seemed to need or awareness of the historical issues that Robert was addressing.

To live and work together with respect, we need to recognize and acknowledge that each of us brings our history with us. We continually filter others' behavior through our own frame of reference and our ongoing experience. For example, the neighborhood we grew up in, our age, nationality, racial and ethnic identities, education, religion, family, and so on, open and close possibilities for us and affect the decisions we make.

Respecting others who are different from ourselves takes understanding ourselves first. By identifying our beliefs, preferences, biases, and prejudices, we are better able to allow others the space and right to experience life from a different perspective. We can listen to ourselves and others both in the moment and from the perspective of history. We can learn and expand our knowledge, awareness, understanding, and more importantly our humanity.

This brings us to the third domain, language. We're hardly aware that we speak of what's "out there" as if it were an objective reality rather than dependent on the observer of that reality. Much of the time we can agree on what we observe. Particularly within our own culture, we share a common way of seeing that serves us in our concerns for coordinating our actions with one another. We are prone to misunderstandings when we don't acknowledge this and stay mired in our exclusive possession of "the truth." Truth then becomes a moral issue when we personalize our differences and pass judgment on the observer.

We generate reality through language, the third domain, and *that* reality generates us. Our reality, expressed through language, drives our actions and reactions. Dr. Humberto Maturana, noted Chilean biologist and expert in cognition has written, "Everything that is said is said by someone."

I was committed to the larger task of providing our client with the best we could possibly offer together. I stated at the beginning of the conversation that I wanted to be vulnerable, to learn while teaching, and to provide an environment that could serve as a laboratory for exploration. As I worked on the design of the presentation with Robert, he agreed to co-present a role-play of our original communication breakdown event, though to do so would make him feel very uncomfortable. Beneath our commitment for one another is a deep regard and respect we each have for who that "someone" is that Maturana refers to.

We also recognize the power of language available to us for co-generating possibilities for the future. Agreements are invented in conversation together and move us from the present to the future by virtue of our saying so. However, agreements also depend on respect and trust. Though we don't necessarily share our private thoughts about the degree of respect and trust we have; these critical judgments we make arise in language that correlate to the actions we take as a result.

Each domain that we touched on can be distinguished. They also intersect. We are always biological, historical, and linguistic beings. Where these domains intersect, the "Heart of the Matter" resides. Who we are *and who we can be* in our infinite unfolding together and individually, is the heart of the matter. Being human goes beyond what we have in the present, in our bodies, through history, and through the identity we build in our conversations together. It is a matter of who we choose to become and what we choose to create together.

The following questions are opportunities for self and group reflection. They can be useful for distinguishing issues that interfere with respect. For the sake of continuing an analysis of our communication breakdown, Robert and I have each responded to the questions.

Questions for Self and Group Reflection

Biology
During our conversation breakdown, did I...

...experience tension in by body?

Joy: Yes, I felt exhausted and had a tightness in my neck and shoulders.

Robert: Yes.

...feel compassion?

Joy: No, I felt confusion and frustration. I also felt sad.

Robert: Yes, when Joy began to cry. Prior to that I felt rushed and agitated.

...feel safe to speak honestly?

Joy: Yes, I had no hidden agenda.

Robert: No.

...pause before responding under stress?

Joy: No, I was wound up as tight as a wire.

Robert: Only toward the end of the conversation.

...feel violated?

Joy: Yes. When Robert said that he didn't feel respected, I felt as though my soul had been stabbed.

Robert: Yes, when Joy compared me to Mel and Sandra.

History

During the conversation, was I...

...aware of how I perceived the other?

Joy: Yes. During the conversation I perceived Robert as not interested in my ideas for the presentation. Then I sensed that he was angry about a previous situation.

Robert: Yes. I had mixed feelings about how I perceived Joy.

...aware of how I was perceived by the other?

Joy: Yes. Robert was clear when he stated that he didn't feel respected by me. Prior to this situation I felt Robert respected me and my work. He had written a letter to that effect several weeks earlier.

Robert: Yes, until she compared me to our two colleagues.

...allowing past situations to rule the present or affect my responses?

Joy: Not in the beginning. However, when he made the statement about respect, I then brought past positive behaviors of other associates into our conversation.

Robert: Yes. I *embodied* the frustration I brought onto the call.

...able to shed the past and create the future?

Joy: Yes. When I said that I couldn't continue to discuss the situation.

Robert: Yes, when I deliberately chose to let go of the issues between us and proposed to start over again on another call.

Language

During the conversation, did I...

...blame the other for the communication breakdown?

Joy: Yes and no. I was tired and just wanted to end the conversation when it was clear we were going nowhere. When I felt blamed by Robert, I then shamed him by bringing up Mel.

Robert: Yes. I blamed Joy for speaking so fast and rushing right into her ideas. I also blamed myself for not following what she was saying.

...insist upon my explanations, beliefs, opinions, and so on, as the absolute truth?

Joy: No.

Robert: Yes, initially.

...command and demand or invite and acknowledge?

Joy: No. I retreated into myself. I wanted this conversation to end.

Robert: No.

...forgive the other?

Joy: No, not during the conversation. I needed time to regroup and figure out what had happened. Later, during our presentation, I apologized to Robert for any suffering I caused him.

Robert: No. I thought that the relationship was probably over.

...see my role in co-creating the situation?

Joy: Absolutely. In my striving to keep my promises, I called Robert only to fulfill the promise and request another time to discuss the presentation. [We do bad things thinking we are doing good things, and we do good things thinking we are doing bad things.]

Robert: Yes. I did not communicate by building frustration with Joy. I also realized, from something she said, that I could be inflexible and hard to work with.

A New Beginning: A Way to Co-Create the Future

Robert and I have an exciting opportunity to shorten the gap between our intentions and our observable behaviors. Let us explore the following questions:

What were our intentions during the conversation?

Joy: My intention was to fulfill my promise to call, to share my ideas and new insight regarding the upcoming presentation, to listen to Robert's ideas, to give and receive feedback on the ideas, and to schedule another meeting by phone when I was rested. I got my energy from my excitement to share a new possibility for teaching a challenging topic.

Robert: My intention was to be on track to design the program and take care of some outstanding issues with Joy. I felt anxious about the upcoming program, then resentful, frustrated, and powerless over the breakdown that occurred.

What were our observable behaviors?

Joy: Robert's observable behaviors were frustration in the tone of his voice and anxiety, which he showed when he switched the issue from presentation ideas to blaming me for not faxing him notes prior to sending them to the client. I also heard confusion, demands, and lack of interest in his voice. there was no evidence in his voice or words about his feelings regarding the new possibilities for presenting our work to our audience.

Robert: I saw Joy as fatigued, overwhelmed, and rushed.

What was our outcome?

We had a complete communication breakdown with little if any respect for or from each other.

What did this outcome allow us to do/become?

We gained the opportunity to become:

- more open and honest with ourselves and each other
- more tolerant
- more intimate

- more observant of our histories and how we are blindly driven to react
- more observant of our bodies
- more willing to continue our relationship on a more honest level
- better at exploring further the ways we represent the best and the worst of human behaviors

Learning and Opportunities

Our belief is that relationships are the key to our learning and growing individually and collectively.

When we are in relationship with someone, we are afforded a very rich opportunity to step outside of ourselves and be influenced by another's perception of the world. We can be with another from his or her point of view and suspend judgment. We can be patient and allow the other person a safe space in which to express him or herself. We can learn about our strengths and weaknesses in the process. For example, the drama we recounted for you was an excellent way for us to question our competence in listening.

Robert and I were able to retreat to our common ground, that is, our care for and concern about one another and our commitment to deliver an extraordinary program for our customer. That ground we stood on together was solid enough for us to let go of our individual egos. We recognized we could convert our situation into an opportunity. Thus, we decided to share our communication breakdown in the program itself and continue to learn and grow from and with each other, in the process.

Thanks for listening.....................
Love,
Joy

James R. Calvin, assistant professor and director of the Johns Hopkins University leadership development program, focuses his research and teaching on reflective leadership and management practice within organizations, experiential games for learning, and strategic leadership for community development. He is examining synergistic relationships that are operative in change efforts and the use of reflective practice to enhance capacity through adaptation and innovation. Calvin's publications have appeared in journals and monographs and he participates in national and international symposia, and has been a consultant to several organizations in the public and private sectors.

Calvin has an extensive background nationally in the development and delivery of curricula for engaging in leadership inquiry and practice. Finally, he was on a team that developed and implemented a national curriculum that promotes collaborative leadership practice within and between organizations that serve youth, families, and communities.

17

Leadership Diversity

James R. Calvin

Biological diversity is the key to the maintenance of the world as we know it. Life in a local site struck down by a passing storm springs back quickly: opportunistic species rush in to fill the spaces. They entrain the succession that circles back to something resembling the original state of the environment

—Edward O. Wilson

Diversity Is Life Itself

About twenty-five years ago the most popular song in America and in many other countries went "I'd like to teach the world to sing in perfect harmony." The song was actually an advertising jingle, and the product was the soft drink Coca-Cola. Yes, the event was staged, but it personified the inclusion and richness of diversity of people in the world. As I reflect further on the message it sent, I see an expression of attitude as the uniting factor that brought the range of humanity together around a common purpose. The desired reality in this setting was an image of respect and camaraderie among people rather than an emphasis on racial division and ideological polarization.

Moving toward the present, I see that coalescing people around a common purpose still remains elusive and that broad public will is a lever to action for honoring diversity and for sharing knowledge and resources that are universal requirements for life and future prosperity in the world. The pursuit of a meaningful living in a shared power world has become more complex because principles of equity conflict with policies and actions around the globe while all stakeholders must deal with the issues related to race, gender, culture, and class that challenge us.

Among the questions we are still seeking answers to as a diverse people are, "What do we have in common?" and "What kinds of traditions bind us together?" Moreover, "What are some of the major obstacles confronting business, government, and social organizations that impede and prevent dialogue, creativity, commitment, and the instituting of policies that support organizational and community renewal by recognizing and accessing diversity?" Honoring diversity means moving toward a culture of long-lasting relationships and partnerships, and this is both cultural and attitudinal. To do so, it is necessary to take steps to develop mechanisms for arriving at serious dialogue and commitment to devise and implement broad policy in support of workforce diversity through learning strategies that assist organizations and governments to encourage relationships that are simultaneously high quality and partnering for extending human capacity.

Establishing criteria and a credible time line for meeting specific goals is very important so that new methodologies and approaches regarding processes designed to change work and working relationships in organizations can be effective. In this vein, there needs to be a concertizing of actions involving the exploration of attitudes and philosophical and cultural approaches to learning that are used by organizations in preparing a highly skilled workforce. The new and adapted strategies and innovations that are emerging should be values driven, mutually fulfilling, and reenergizing to sufficiently tap diversity as an asset.

Moreover, this will involve risk taking, common visioning, and planned actions that will become essential practice for transforming culture systems and decision-making processes in organizations and communities both locally and globally.

There are many attitudes and conflicting actions that must be confronted on a daily basis, such as individual belief systems that do not mesh around a common whole. Mark Gerzon, author of *A Home Divided,* expresses the view that six belief systems are fighting each other in America (religion, capitalism, disempowerment, media, transformation, and governance), and these actions are disuniting the nation. It is important to note that similar issues and challenges of disunity are being faced by nations in Europe, Africa, and in the Pacific Rim. Thus, as the twenty-first century dawns, the widening and deepening embrace of diversity is a key to our common future because diversity has always been an integral part of nature and natural order in the world.

With this thought in mind, my intent is to provide some reflections and feedback in support of current methods and potential future strategies and interventions that can become models to enable diversity to be focused and unleashed creatively in all types of organizations. In doing so, we face the long-term challenges of melding perspectives into a wider acceptance that racial, ethnic, and gender diversity share a common denominator—that of humans striving toward achievement and purpose.

At first glance the harnessing of diverse mindsets and energies might appear to be a good thing to do as well as a simple task to accomplish.

However, given the current reality of learning and adapting knowledge and new skills acquisition for greater capacity, there is a paradox in effect because work and life systems are still going through downsizing, rightsizing, reengineering, and other restructuring events at the behest of organizations and governments.

The Will of Diversity

In view of the preceding depiction, I refer to Peter Drucker's mention that "no century in recorded history has experienced so many social transformations and such radical ones as the twentieth century." Drucker's mention of current models of work and organizational configurations provides timely insights for thinking about and grappling with a plethora of issues that revolve around the inequality in knowledge and skills challenging a growing workforce diversity in America and other nations as ways are sought to foster cooperation while meeting competitive pressures.

The expansive question of managing diversity is very deep and potent, and it requires long-term thinking to implement comprehensive strategies and actions for transforming and re-building future organizations and communities. Founder of the American Institute for Managing Diversity, R. Roosevelt Thomas, Jr., has also asked several defining questions: "Given the competitive environment we face and the diverse workforce we have, are we getting the highest productivity possible? Does our system work as smoothly as it could? Is morale as high as we would wish? And are those things as strong as they would be if all the people who worked here were the same sex and race and nationality and had the same lifestyle and value system and way of working?

If the answers are no, then the solution is to substitute positive for negative aspects. That means changing the system and modifying the core culture." We thus require visioning, perseverance, and comprehensive planning for inculcating meaningful events that lead to transformations in the lives of stakeholders. Furthermore, this drive for improving the quality of intraorganizational working relationships derives from viewing diversity as a value added for partnering that accrues because the principle of lifelong learning is as an essential element for human, organization, and community renewal. Lifelong learning is equally important for maintaining balance, growth, equanimity, and attitude.

The potential breakthroughs and subsequent payoff is a high stakes reservoir of highly skilled human problem-solving capital that can be extended through technology as new connections for commerce is made on all continents. A major contributing factor in this chain of events is the element of public will and trust during an era of immense change that continues to buffet all systems and living environments.

What is happening is a worldwide shift in paradigms for doing business and maintaining communities, and this phenomenon is influencing the desires, goals, and capabilities of many organizations and nations to promote healthy and thriving global enterprise and communities.

We know from consultant and bestselling author Joel Barker and others that when a paradigm shifts, there are two cutting actions that take place at the same time: The first is that we see what we agree with and want to see both individually and collectively; the second is that it is hard for us to see what we do not agree with and do not want to see.

In the United States, and in other highly developed nations, these issues are further impacted by different cultures and lifestyles and the mixing of cultures that has occurred in recent years as diverse people enter the workforce with a variety of skills. A defining view of this occurrence is represented by each ten-year census, which acts as a lens to tell us who we are becoming as Americans.

This dynamic factor is the growth and expansion of diversity; it is a potent force that is helping to drive major change in the workplace and in the society. The demographer Harold "Bud" Hodgkinson tells a story about growing diversity: In 1960 there were two categories, black and white. By the 1990 census there were more than forty racial and ethnic group identifications. This number will be increased significantly by the year 2000 census because there will be even more racial and ethnic choices for people to declare. Hodgkinson asks what it means. One meaning is that it is a much broader question beyond black or white when describing population groups. Group diversity, identification, and membership is at times confusing, and it is a persistent challenge for organizations as they seek to navigate across cultures.

Yet another compounding set of questions is: Who make up these new groups? What skills and knowledge do they bring to the table? What should they be able to do in organizations and in communities and the larger community? What sorts of new dimensions and ways for sharing power and resources are necessary? One approach is to institute culturally based sensitivity and responsiveness as a method for growing healthy cultures in organizations. A second approach is to respect, share, and align values. In this vein, the promoting of responsive cultures recognizes the dualism of respecting and valuing diversity as central to the purpose and goals of the organization and also as parallel lifestyle and culture systems that work together synergistically.

The question of values clarification and congruence helps to define an attitude in an organization, and it is a critical set of steps along the pathway to embracing different personal values. To this point, consultant Frances E. Kendall and many others have said that differences matter and should be recognized and valued in order to create workplaces where people are appreciated *and rewarded*. Again, this is vitally essential practice to engage in if business, government, and social organizations in the United States and around the world want to invest in prosperity and good health for the coming years.

Several Diversity Stories and Situations

An old adage goes something like this—it is never easy to move heaven and earth. Likewise, it is not easy to scale a mountain, nor is it easy to move a mountain. Consequently, pursuing an active commitment to diversity is a long-term affair heaped with many challenges, pitfalls, and potential roadblocks and setbacks. Yet, to tap human diversity is also to gain access to the power of an enduring source of ideas, creativity, and energy for organizational renewal and transformation, and it ought to be a primary task and goal we strive to make a common reality. Yes, there are choices and directions and paths to travel, and collectively we can figure out which options to choose. When will we make the right choices?

I recently attended an American Management Association breakfast seminar where the keynoter described the bright efficacy of affinity group development over a six-year period at a Johnson & Johnson subsidiary in New Jersey. There was a clear articulation of a perceived and understood need to create a vision for change, set goals, and engage in risk taking for deriving some of the potential benefits that come from enhanced diversity. Furthermore, there were some universal lessons that had been learned and some old realities were again confirmed concerning this revolutionary approach to fostering new working relationships.

Briefly, minorities and women had never been empowered as full partners in the organization, as evidenced by their not being in pipeline positions that would lead to future advancement into senior management ranks in the organization. The experience of affinity group learning was valuable because ample attention was given to group identity by not painting everybody with the same broad brushstroke of uniformity.

The intent of this strategy of nurturing and then bringing together different affinity groups was to do some sharing and common visioning in relation to the mission of the organization. It was reported that after six years, a malleable empowerment strategy had improved outcomes for several women who were moving upward in the organization but not at all for African Americans, who had not been inserted into the pipeline. Thus, the depth and severity of the blockage is further amplified by intransigence when organizational cultures resist change even when there are good reasons and general agreement that an organization will be better off and greatly improved in its ability to reach its competitive goals when there is a high level of inclusion involving diverse problem solvers and decision makers.

The commitment, transfer, and use of this valuable knowledge as a constructive tool by the parent organization can promote future opportunities for its entire workforce. If the choices made are in the affirmative, then the firmament will support and allow for the growth of firm roots that ultimately will extend widely inside and outside the organization.

However, there is the possibility that another direction can be taken by this organization to begin fully accessing some of the many benefits of diversity. So, the question becomes what and where is the common ground? What must organizations do to promote common ground experiences, and how do organizations decide to move forward constructively and cohesively after people have traveled from different directions and paths to the same point in space and time?

Some organizations know from experience that it is good business to recognize different and divergent cultures, values, and ways to make decisions for doing problem solving and work.

In Chicago, Illinois, I facilitated a learning and team-building activity with a racially, ethnically, and gender diverse group of twelve people who were participating in a citywide leadership development program for middle managers. We were actively engaged in a simulation designed to encourage partnering, teamwork, and the sharing of power among people from different backgrounds and from different parts of the city. The communication and team-building work of the group was evident because members had been together for several months and had grown measurably.

One African-American woman in the group had emerged as a strong-willed and strong-armed individual who kicked, yanked, and jerked the other team members on several occasions. She even drew a small amount of blood from another group member, a white male who headed a Hispanic community organization. When we debriefed the team power sharing activity, the African-American woman said that she was sending a signal that she could be counted on to take the lead when it was necessary, and she had no intent to hurt anybody.

The white male responded that he had thought briefly about matching forces with the woman but had chosen instead to follow her lead because he thought that others in the group might be hurt by his proposed actions and good intentions (and he mentioned that he really had no quick plan to change the outcome). We discussed the attempts at partnering, the conflict, the avoidance of conflict, and what could have been done to get closer to common ground for sharing power. Since the power sharing simulation and experience, the team has spent more than a year learning and sharing together and has started to tackle some tough issues under an umbrella of race and community diversity in several Chicago communities. This small effort is very important given the ongoing history of race relations in Chicago and in other cities. If it is viewed only in global proportions, it might appear isolated and not relevant.

The potential for broader human diversity is that there are many initiatives underway that involve the quality and type of effort in Chicago. A primary goal is to enhance the capacity of organizations by encouraging diverse leadership who can confront deep concerns and overcome obstacles while managing change processes. In thinking about what works and what doesn't for preparing and advancing diverse leaders, Ann Morrison suggests, "To plan and conduct an effective diversity effort, organizations need a framework that provides a broad perspective and that makes relevant recommendations for all gender and ethnic groups."

As I think about developing broader perspectives on diversity in the workplace, I can see several trends in action. The first is that smart organizations are seeking to build workplace diversity beyond a level-one approach, which is recognition and appreciation. Workforce diversity at level two is an expansion of efforts to build greater organizational capacity through people, and this can be an enduring source as the workplace changes in coming years. I further envision that smart organizations will want to employ strategies that promote opportunities for pipelining racially and gender diverse leadership for increased representation and mobility at middle and top levels in organizations in anticipation of continuing global shift. Moreover, the recently released Federal Glass Ceiling Commission report *Good for Business: Making Full Use of the Nation's Human Capital* is further impetus to establish a real pipeline for advancement.

Mining Diversity Is an Olympic Challenge

Diversity will continue expanding widely while many organizations and governments are contracting, if not altering, shrinking, and sometimes disappearing in response to worldwide economic and social pressures.

Another outcome of diversity is the blending and distilling of talents and then tapping into these higher-order skills for common benefit in an organization or community. However, if the perception of diversity is to limit its capacity for interconnectedness, then the quality and consistency of outcomes will more than likely be less sharing, more indifference, and a cloudy and uncertain common future.

In view of the preceding, I want to tell another brief story that is drawn from my work with diverse leaders, managers, and citizens who live and work throughout the United States. These leaders, managers, and citizens are working in business, education, health, social services, youth development, government, and not-for-profit organizations. A personal credo for engaging in this partnership work with others is to have a healthy attitude about others because we are all connected across systems, and a major portion of combined effort is to give and get respect and to develop trust and capacity for common visioning. Applying these criteria are essential for engaging in collaborative enterprise by a community of people. Thus, the character and quality of this kind of interaction is based on cultural adaptation toward consensus that allows for the acquisition and use of knowledge and skills and the establishment of learning communities to meet common needs through interdependence.

A healthy attitude is very important for maintaining active involvement in endeavors that foster change processes to open and widen the receptiveness of organizational cultures and systems.

The intent of many of systemic change initiatives is to improve and enhance the capacity and ability of education, employment, health, and social service systems to proactively impact the quality of life for diverse people.

For the past ten years I have played poker with a diverse cast of individuals who are engaged in a leadership development program that prepares diverse leaders for the nation. When we begin a game, we set rules and determine the stakes for all participants. Attitudinally, our overarching goal and premise for playing is to challenge our individual and collective thinking about the purpose, means, and capability of leadership for visioning and doing problem solving that is related to real life issues that need solutions. So, for those of us who have chosen to indulge in poker, the usual rules of the game that generally ensure at least one winner do not apply. Our rules for playing poker are designed to facilitate conversation and strategy. Winning only occurs when we are able to share something valuable within our operating culture for collaboration. Oh yes, the games are fun. Of more importance to us regarding diversity is dialogue around the question of how we share in bringing together and building resources for action and then spread the products and profits.

Taylor H. Cox, Jr.'s authoritative study presents a cogent view on the efficacy and spreading of diversity as organizational capital. Cox presents accurate reasons why organizational flexibility is enhanced when members of minority groups become true partners who add cognitive value to an organization because a higher level of innovative and adaptive thinking is created, which is needed for doing business. Cox states, "The process of changing organizational cultures is a long-term and difficult process." Yet, many organizations remain slow in the face of present realities to begin to take advantage of developmental strategies and approaches through diversity that will augment decision-making efficacy, which triggers other tangible outcomes for the organization. Another principle for organizations to consider is the rate at which there is a need to continuously adapt for flexibility and creativity in a shifting environment. What was done yesterday will not necessarily work today. This is also an indicator of who has access and who doesn't have access in organizations. I am reminded of Peter Drucker's notion of "the new society of organizations...a society where knowledge is the primary resource for individuals and for the economy overall." This will be not be a simple task since knowledge power has to be cultivated and shared between people and groups in order to be beneficial. Still, it is a goal worth pursuing because it provides hope for a better future.

Thus, my role has been a combination of learning, participating, co-laboring, coaching, and sometimes teaching when working with groups to crystallize cultural and personal issues into clarity toward a common interest. I view this as attitude bridging, which enables diverse people to achieve real dialogue, identify complimentary styles, and then begin building on a foundation for learning and sharing by co-laboring together.

Some Final Thoughts on Leadership Attitude, Diversity, and Shared Power

In late November 1995, I had an opportunity to meet at length with U.S. Olympic Committee President Dr. Leroy T. Walker, and I asked him what he meant by leadership attitude as we talked about the 1996 Olympic Games to be held in Atlanta, Georgia. I wanted to gain a broader understanding of what he thought the Olympics symbolized and meant for diversity and groups working together in Atlanta. We started our conversation in a cab ride to the hotel where Walker would be making an evening keynote presentation to several hundred leaders from around the nation.

Walker responded to my question by saying that "leadership attitude is how people see things...furthermore, we cannot afford to lose the talent that should go into the circle...this means the range of ideas and possibilities within an organization as represented by the diversity of groups." Walker elaborated on leadership attitude by saying that widening the pool of people who participated as idea generators and decision makers was essential to bringing the Olympic games to Atlanta in 1996. Moreover, the $1.7 billion dollar organization that was created to mount the Atlanta games was built on a foundation of trust and confidence between diverse people that was achieved through dialogue, open thinking, and a shared commitment to building and sharing resources with the whole community.

Clearly, what will take place after the Olympics in Atlanta is of greater importance. Will the relationships hold, and will the modified behavior lead to new possibilities? Or will the culture return to doing business as before? As we talked further, it became clear that the drive toward mounting a successful Olympics did not mean that there were no failures along the way, but that failures are part of a long journey. It takes years to achieve success and especially so when the outcome is the Olympic games with broad universal appeal and the uniting of human spirit. What is important here is not the overt commercialism and intense competition and nationalism that is often present but a sense of genuine unity.

The principle of leadership attitude is a key factor in connecting and elucidating the enormous potential of diversity regarding ideas and strategies for making work more creative and productive in conjunction with living life to greater satisfaction.

If organizations are to become and remain healthy and vibrant, they will require a diversity of people who work together and who are highly skilled to take the journey to success. My friend Neil Postman offers an idea of diversity "as being an inclusive narrative and...the story that tells of how our interactions with many kinds of people make us who we are...furthermore, it helps to explain the past, give clarity to the present, and provide guidance for the future." As stated earlier, one strength of accessing diversity is an extension in capacity that enhances the capability of whole organizations to manage change and prosper in changing environments.

As organizations continue to swim and drift against the stormy and raging currents of dynamic change, the efficacy and benefits of diversity for organization and community renewal is ready to be unleashed now and in coming years as we enter into the twenty-first century. Let's move forward by doing what is necessary to make it happen.

John O'Neil was president of California School of Professional Psychology from 1978 to 1996. His new position is president of the Center for Leadership Renewal located in the San Francisco Presidio. Prior to his career in higher education, he worked at AT&T and in venture capital.

Following the publication of his book *The Paradox of Success* in 1995,he has spent increasing time lecturing, and giving workshops and consultations to organizations on the subject of leadership. He has a new book, *Leadership Aikido* on the subject of long-distance leaders and the practices that allow them to remain productive and creative.

O'Neil is also active as a member of, and advisor to, several board of directors. He is currently serving on the board of Hanna Andersson Clothing Company, E-marketing Partners, Venture Strategy, and Neighborhood America.

18

A View from the Trenches

John O'Neil

Much of the current controversy surrounding diversity and higher education, particularly its legislative side, affirmative action, misses the point. Whatever righteousness one might feel for or against affirmative action, the fact is no professional educational program can achieve distinction without cultural and intellectual diversity.

- Without cultural and intellectual diversity, any contemporary education of professionals is simply out of touch with the reality those professionals will face in the world.

- Without cultural and intellectual diversity, research efforts will have limited applicability in an increasingly diverse world.

- Without cultural and intellectual diversity, professional services will not reach many of those most in need and will not be effective and appropriate.

We at the California School of Professional Psychology (CSPP) have learned over the past twenty-five years that diversity is not something that can be achieved by good intentions alone; it is a difficult, ongoing, ever-changing process that requires commitment, leadership, openness to change, and continual reevaluation. But diversity is also the lifeblood that keeps an institution open to the new ideas and perspectives that make it relevant to the society it serves.

CSPP's charter was fashioned in 1969 in response to universities shutting down clinical programs, thus cutting off a future generation of service providers. The school's founders, leaders in the field who had been trained in distinguished research institutions, believed that psychological research should be informed and refined by clinical experience. Their vision was a school that would focus on training clinical psychologists who could provide the highest quality psychological services to people who needed them. Its faculty would include outstanding practitioners who would mentor students and provide them with hands-on, carefully supervised clinical experience. From the very beginning it attracted people committed to serving their communities. In its first year, CSPP's faculty taught without salary. Its first student cohort insisted that part of their tuition be set aside for scholarships.

CSPP is a very different institution than it was in 1969. Its commitment to highest quality professional training to meet community needs is unchanged, but it has developed and matured in ways that its founders could not have imagined. From a storefront in Los Angeles furnished with beanbag chairs, it has developed into a four-campus system: San Francisco (now Alameda) was established in 1970, San Diego in 1972, and Fresno in 1973. Each campus has a comprehensive library collection, and technological and other facilities for faculty, staff, and students are continually upgraded. In 1992 CSPP awarded 17.2 percent of the clinical and organizational psychology doctoral degrees in the United States. However, one of the most significant changes is CSPP's commitment to diversity in program development, faculty and student recruitment, service delivery, and strategic planning.

When I assumed presidency of the school in 1977, there were only a few ethnic minority and women faculty members, and the student body was far from diverse. This was in large part a reflection of the cultural milieu in higher education at that time; the pools of doctoral prospects also reflected those circumstances. However, the psychological literature was increasingly demonstrating that diagnoses and treatment could be seriously flawed when psychologists were not cognizant of and sensitive to the cultural backgrounds of their patients. How could the school fulfill its mission of training clinicians who would provide the best possible psychological services to a culturally diverse community, especially in California, if the school's curriculum, training, and educational policies were dominated by white males? We also questioned how our institution could remain healthy if it was not representative of the general population around it and thus meet the real needs of that population.

The Leadership Team

The first task was to develop a leadership team that was committed to achieving cultural diversity. We were extremely fortunate to already have on board some dedicated people, many of whom are now the primary leaders of the institution and members of the President's Council, which includes the four chancellors, two vice presidents, and three departmental directors and is the principal advisory body to the president. After we found the right initial team, recruiting other people who shared our vision became a much easier task The team embraced diversity as a primary value for three reasons: (1) in a democratic society, access to employment, education, and public services of all its citizens is a moral imperative; (2) in a nation as culturally diverse as the United States (especially in California where by the year 2000 more than 50 percent of the population will be non-white), a well-educated workforce is essential to its ability to compete in the global economy; and (3) it would foster a much more vibrant, creative place for people to work and study. In all our programs—clinical psychology, organizational psychology, and community service—we hoped to supply the community with practitioners who could provide clinical and community services to a culturally diverse population and assist organizations in developing workplace environments that enhance the creativity and productivity of all their employees. Also, it became clear that making diversity part of our educational training activities was essential to the capacity of our graduates to provide ethical and competent services to an increasingly multicultural client population.

A School with Unusual Governance

The board of trustees, made up of leaders drawn from psychology, business, and the community, has ultimate responsibility for the policy, direction, and management of the school.

And, unlike other institutions of higher education, four faculty and four student representatives (one from each of the school's four campuses) also serve on the board of trustees. Their presence was another strength in helping us to move the diversity agenda forward.

The Importance of Explaining, Selling, Staying the Course

The next goal was to achieve the "critical mass" of minority faculty and students, the 15 percent that many authorities feel is essential before minorities feel comfortable or are even capable of participating in affecting the institutional culture. There were concerns among faculty and some board members that adding diversity to hiring and admission criteria would dilute quality and harm the school's academic reputation. The school's leadership believed that diversity was a basic *element* of the quality of the faculty and student body, but concerns had to be addressed. The school's leaders began to sell a powerful ally, the Western Association of Schools and Colleges, on diversity as a criteria for accreditation. The American Psychological Association began to take notice of diversity in its accreditation site visits. Unfortunately, accreditation is not only imprecise in its application of "standards," but it also often operates with its own shadows and hidden biases.

CSPP was fortunate to have several visionary leaders on the board of trustees, including Gordon Sherman, president and CEO of Midas Muffler International, who had demonstrated that putting muffler shops in minority neighborhoods was an astute business decision. The lesson of his experience was that criticism and alternative points of view need to be honored, but in the final analysis it is up to the leadership to do the right things and find solutions to problems raised by questioning voices. CSPP's leadership team listened to concerns about diversity and addressed them by expanding the pool of minority student and faculty candidates.

Strategies for Recruiting and Retaining Minority Students and Faculty

There were significant obstacles to recruiting minority faculty and students. The pool of minority faculty member candidates was extraordinarily small, and other higher education institutions with much greater resources were fishing the same waters. The competition for students was also great. In addition, CSPP was something of a maverick in the predominantly research-focused culture of higher education, and advisers to minority graduate students entering the job market would steer candidates for faculty positions to more "prestigious" research institutions. There was a similar problem in getting minority students from undergraduate institutions to apply to CSPP. The school employed a number of strategies, and these have produced steady increases in faculty and student diversity.

- CSPP could not compete with heavily endowed private or tax-supported public universities for senior minority faculty in the field by offering competitive salary and benefits packages, but it could expand the pool of candidates by looking at less experienced candidates.

- It sought the help of partners, such as the American Psychological Association, California state colleges, and others, to identify especially promising faculty and student candidates. CSPP faculty, some of whom also taught at other institutions, utilized their personal and professional networks to recruit outstanding minority faculty and students.

- It developed cooperative agreements with undergraduate institutions for minority graduates, such as California state universities, Fresno Pacific University, and others.

- Inquiries by minority students were followed up with personal phone calls—sometimes from CSPP faculty or staff, sometimes by current CSPP minority students or alumni.

- Catalogs, recruitment, and other descriptive brochures all stressed CSPP's commitment to diversity and set forth the benefits it offers to minority students: a supportive community, course offering, special assistance.

- CSPP has a flexible admissions policy and offered pre-enrollment and ongoing assistance programs to all students to upgrade skills necessary for success in the program. Students' progress was continually monitored throughout their time at CSPP and special counseling and assistance were provided when needed.

- Minority students and new minority faculty members, wherever possible and desirable, were assigned experienced minority faculty mentors.
- A tremendous obstacle to higher education for many minority students is not having sufficient financial resources. In 1979 CSPP instituted a policy of devoting 1 percent of its annual tuition revenues to minority scholarships; it now commits 2 percent. CSPP's success in achieving faculty and curriculum diversity and providing excellent education for minority students has been recognized by funding agencies, and in 1994 it was able to offer substantial scholarships from a variety of other sources (in addition to funds from research and service grants, field placement stipends, and teaching and research assistantships).
- Each campus established an emphasis area with a multicultural education and training focus involving curriculum, field training, and research experiences dealing with ethnic minority populations.

Diversity and the Provision of Quality Service to Students and the Community

As Midas Muffler had experienced, CSPP found that new markets for its services, as well as access to other resources, were made available *because* it was an institution that honored and was respected for the diversity of its faculty, student body, curriculum, and programs. For example, it was successful in obtaining foundation support. The James Irvine Foundation gave a $275,000 grant for its Multicultural, Intergenerational Program, and CSPP raised $300,000 in matching funds from outside sources over the next two years; in 1990 the Fund for the Improvement of Postsecondary Education gave a grant to integrate multicultural issues into every course, to name just two. CSPP was also able to market its services to business organizations and public agencies.

The leadership team decided at the outset that cultural diversity would be integrated into every aspect of the school. Mistakes were made and there were out-and-out failures, but we learned to not judge our mistakes and failures associated with diversity by a higher standard than we used for other decisions— sometimes we made mistakes in admitting students or hiring faculty from the dominant culture, and minority hiring and admissions decisions were not immune. All mistakes had to be dealt with in ways that demonstrated fairness to the school as a whole. And we learned from all of our mistakes.

We believe that CSPP now has an outstanding faculty who through its race, gender, age, physical challenges, and sexual orientation represent broad diversity. Researchers at the University of Indiana ranked *Counseling the Culturally Different (2nd Ed.)*, co-authored by CSPP's Derald Sue and his brother, David Sue, at the top of their list of publications on multicultural counseling. The quality of its training is confirmed when CSPP students compete nationally for American Psychological Association pre-doctoral internships at prestigious institutions—Yale, Baylor College of Medicine, numerous Veterans Administration hospitals, New York University Medical Center, University of Texas Health Sciences Center, and La Rabida Children's Hospital and Research Center. CSPP graduates have higher than average passing rates in both written and oral California licensing exams.

How Diversity Is Expanding and Transforming the Field

The field of psychology is changing dramatically. No longer are psychologists only in independent practice conducting individual therapy. They also provide psychotherapeutic services to dysfunctional families; increase the quality of life for the chronically ill, brain-injured patients, and the elderly; decrease drug or alcohol dependence for those with substance abuse problems; and teach an understanding of individual and societal behavior. In addition, they uncover new knowledge through research where it is most needed—involving people with AIDS or single-parent families; performing personnel assessments and developing plans for managing organizational growth in corporations; and running healthy behavior seminars for business's employee assistance programs. They work at policy setting executive levels in city hall, the state houses, and corporate headquarters.

CSPP is in the business of eliminating psychological barriers and creating communities and environments that aid the development of our most significant national resource, a diverse population. CSPP's Fresno chancellor, Mary Beth Kenkel, has said that the purpose of professional psychology is to "give it away," to transmit the knowledge and insights it has gained to the wider community. The diversity of CSPP's faculty and student body has greatly enhanced its capacity to do this.

- In conjunction with the Montebello Unified School District, Professor Sam Chan, director of the Professional Services Center at CSPP Los Angeles, has created a program in which CSPP students provide multicultural competency training to thirty-three administrators within the school district.

- The Professional Services Center also has a $400,000 contract from the Federal Aviation Administration to provide diversity awareness and sexual harassment prevention training to more than six hundred FAA managers and employees over a two-year period.

- Fresno County has become home to more than 50,000 Southeast Asian refugees (10 percent of the population). Despite tremendous efforts to provide social services, educational and vocational training, and mental health programs, many of these residents remain dependent on public assistance. Their adjustment problems are intensified or triggered by the underlying distress of atrocities, starvation, and war they experienced in their homeland.

- CSPP Fresno has a collaborative program with Fresno County, the Southeast Asian Refugee Counseling Service, designed to assist this population. Fresno students are assisting in developing a culturally appropriate instrument for measuring posttraumatic stress disorder symptoms that has been translated into various Southeast Asian languages.

- CSPP San Diego has established, with a $400,000 U.S. Department of Education grant, the Rehabilitation Research and Training Center on Mental Health of Persons Who are Hard of Hearing or Late Deafened to conduct research and improve the accessibility of high-quality services for this population.

- A most exciting new program is the Community Health Relation Institute, directed by Dr. Roger Mills, through the CSPP System Office. It has had remarkable success in alleviating problems of substance abuse, teen pregnancy, crime, domestic violence, and other problems endemic in public housing neighborhoods. Residents who live within these communities learn to develop a collaborative problem-solving process.

CSPP is constantly expanding its definition of diversity and is continually being transformed by these new perspectives.

A final note: As this chapter goes to press, the nation is again being torn asunder by a deeply felt struggle over affirmative action. A primary task of leadership is to help form and reform an organization's value set and then act as the good messenger, one who keeps the values alive and useful. Real success in creating a strong and healthy multicultural society, one that can take its proper place in the global environment of the twenty-first century, will occur when leaders are able to transcend the affirmative action debate and unleash the creativity and productivity inherent in our diversity.

Recommended Reading

Abramms, Bob. *Cultural Diversity Sourcebook*. Amherst, MA: ODT, 1996

Adler, N.J., and George F. Simons (Eds.). *International Dimensions of Organizational Behavior*. Boston: Kent Publishing Company, 1986.

Arrien, Angeles. *The Four-Fold Way: Walking the Paths of the Warrior, Teacher, Healer, and Visionary*. San Francisco: Harper Collins, 1993.

Bates, C. *Pigs Eat Wolves: Going into Partnership With Your Dark Side*. Saint Paul, MN: Yes International Publishers, 1991.

Capra, Fritjof. *The Turning Point: Science, Society, and the Rising Culture*. New York: Bantam Books, 1983

Chesler, M.A. "White Men's Roles in Multicultural Coalitions," in B.P. Bowser & R.G. Hunt (Eds.), *Impacts of Racism on White Americans*, (2nd. ed.,). Thousand Oaks, CA: Sage, 1996.

Chesler, M.A. "Race Talk: Thinking and Talking About Racism," in Diversity Factor 3, no.3 (1995).

Chrislip, David, and Carl E. Larson. *Collaborative Leadership*. San Francisco: Jossey-Bass, 1994.

Cose, E. *A Man's World: How Real is Male Privilege—And How High is Its Price?* New York: Harper Collins, 1995.

Covey, Stephen R. *Seven Habits of Highly Effective People: Restoring the Character Ethic*. New York: Simon and Schuster, 1990.

Cross, E., J.H. Katz, F.A. Miller, and E.W. Seashore. *The Promise of Diversity: Over 40 Voices Discuss Strategies for Eliminating Discrimination in Organizations*. Burr Ridge, IL: Irwin Professional Publishing, 1994.

Cummings, Marlene. *Individual Differences* program. Madison, WI: Wisconsin Department of Public Instruction, 1971.

Eisler, Riane. *The Chalice and The Blade: Our History, Our Future*. San Francisco: Harper & Row, 1987.

Eisler, Riane. *Sacred Pleasure: Sex, Myth, and the Politics of the Body*. San Francisco: Harper San Francisco, 1995.

Eisler, Riane and David Loye. *The Partnership Way: New Tools for Living and Learning*. San Francisco: HarperCollins, 1990.

Eisler, Riane, David Loye, and Kari Norgaard. *Women, Men, and the Global Quality of Life*. Pacific Grove, CA: The Center of Partnership Studies, 1995.

Federal Glass Ceiling Commission. *Good for Business: Making Full Use of the Nation's Human Capital.* Washington, DC, 1995.

Gerzon, Mark. *A Home Divided: Six Belief Systems Struggling for America's Soul*. New York: G.P. Putnam's Sons, 1996.

Gilligan, C. *In a Different Voice: Psychological Theory and Women's Development*. Cambridge, MA: Harvard University Press, 1982.

Gudjkunst, William B. *Bridging Differences*. Newbury Park, CA: Sage Publications, 1991.

Haessly, Jacqueline. "Expanding Our Awareness of Diversity—People with Disabilities," in *The Reporter*, newsletter of the National Council of Family Relations. Minneapolis, MN: December, 1995.

Haessly, Jacqueline. *Learning to Live Together*. San Francisco: Resource Publications, 1989.

Haessly, Jacqueline. "Toward Inclusiveness," in *The Reporter,* newsletter of the National Council of Family Relations. Minneapolis, MN: July, 1994.

Haessly, Jacqueline. *Recovery from Racism* workshop presentation. Cincinnati, OH: The Union Institute, 1996.

Hall, E.T. *Beyond Culture.* New York: Doubleday, 1981.

Hateley, Barbara ("BJ"), and Warren H. Schmidt. *A Peacock in the Land of Penguins: A Tale of Diversity and Discovery.* San Francisco: Berrett-Koehler, 1997.

Hofstede, G. *Culture's Consequences: International Differences in Work Related Values.* Beverly Hills, CA: Sage, 1980.

hooks, bell. *Teaching to Transgress: Education as the Practice of Freedom.* New York: Routledge, 1994.

Janis, I.L., and L. Mann. *Decision Making: A Psychological Analysis of Conflict, Choice, and Commitment.* New York: Free Press, 1977.

Johnson, B. *Polarity Management: Identifying and Managing Unsolvable Problems.* Amherst, MA: HRD Press, Inc., 1992.

Kochman, T. *Black and White Styles in Conflict.* Chicago: The University of Chicago Press, 1981.

Ludeman, Kate. *The Worth Ethic: How to Profit from the Changing Values of the New Work Force.* New York: E.P. Dutton, 1989.

Maturana, H. and Francisco J. Varela. *The Tree of Knowledge.* Boston: Shambala Publications, 1987.

McIntosh, P. *White Privilege and Male Privilege: A Personal Account of Coming to See Correspondences Through Work in Women's Studies,* (Vol. Working Paper #189). Wellesley, MA: Wellesley College, Center for Research on Women, 1988.

Menendez, Diane. *Recovery from Racism* workshop presentation, The Union Institute. Cincinnati, OH: 1996.

Myers, Selma and Jonamay Lambert. *More Diversity Icebreakers,* Amherst, MA: Amherst Educational Publishing, 1996.

Neal, R. "The Conversion of White Men to Equity and Diversity in the Workplace," in *OD Practitioner.* Portland, OR: Organization Development Network, 1993.

Project Understanding, Educational Program, Milwaukee Public Education Forum. Milwaukee, WI: 1967.

Renesch, John and Bill DeFoore. (Eds.). *The New Bottom Line: Bringing Heart and Soul to Business.* San Francisco: New Leaders Press, 1996.

Ritvo, R.A., A.H. Litwin, and L. Butler (Eds.). Managing in the Age of Change. Burr Ridge, IL: Irwin and NTL Institute, 1995.

Schein, E.H. Organizational Culture and Leadership. San Francisco: Jossey-Bass, 1992.

Shelton, C. *The Self-Interest in Diversity for Straight, White American-Born Male Managers.* Seattle, WA: Diversity Management Inc., 1995.

Simons, George F., Bob Abramms, L. Ann Hopkins, and Diane J. Johnson (Eds.). *Cultural Diversity Fieldbook.* Princeton, NJ: Peterson, 1996.

Steele, S. *The Content of Our Character.* New York: St. Martin's Press, 1990.

Tannen, D. *You Just Don't Understand.* New York: William Morrow, 1990.

Terry, R. "Diversity: Curse or Blessing for the Elimination of White Racism?" in B.P. Bowser & R.G. Hunt (Eds.), *Impact on Racism on White Americans* (Second ed.,). Thousand Oaks, CA: Sage, 1996.

Terry, R.W. *Authentic Leadership: Courage in Action.* San Francisco: Jossey- Bass, 1993.

Villena-Mata, Darling. *Recovery from Racism* workshop presentation, The Union Institute. Cincinnati, OH: 1996.

Williams, Clarence. *Recovery from Racism* workshop presentation, The Union Institute. Cincinnati, OH: 1996.

Weaver, G.R. (Ed.), *Readings in Cross-Cultural Communication* (2nd. ed.). Lexington, MA: Ginn Press, 1987.

Wylie, Janet. *Chances and Choices: How Women Can Succeed in Today's Knowledge-Based Businesses.* Vienna, VA: EBW Press, 1996.

Zinn, H. *A People's History of the United States.* New York: Harper Collins, 1980.

How to Contact the Authors and Editor

WENDY S. APPEL
Courageous Communication
2106 Ardis Dr.
San Jose, CA 95125
Tel. 408.265.6944
Fax 408.265.7876
Email: courcom@aol.com

ANGELES ARRIEN
4000 Bridgeway, #316
Sausalito, CA 94966
Tel. 415.331.5050
Fax 415.331.5069
Email: AArrien@aol.com

JAMES R. CALVIN
Organizational Consulting
9545 Ridgeview Dr.
Columbia, MD 21046
Tel. 301.725.8541
Email:
jcalvin@jhuvms.hcf.jhu.edu

JOY CARVER
Carver & Associates
4645 Kempton Place
Marietta, GA 30067
Tel. 770.579.2389
Fax 770.579.2673
Email: pjoycarver@aol.com

DIANNE CRAMPTON
60968 Onyx St.
Bend, OR 97702
Tel. 877.538.2822
Fax 541.312.2806
Email: tigers@ucinet.com

RIANE EISLER
PO Box 51936
Pacific Grove, CA 93950
Tel. 831.624.8337
Fax 831.626.3734
Email:
center@partnershipway.org

DAVID GOFF
A Foundation for
    Interdependence
630 B University Ave.
Palo Alto, CA 94301
Tel. 650.473.0366
Email:
dg@4interdependence.com

MIKHAIL GORBACHEV
The Gorbachev Foundation
The Presidio, Box 29434
San Francisco, CA 94129
Tel. 415.771.4567
Fax 415.771.4443

JACQUELINE HAESSLY
Peacemaking Associates
2437 North Grant Blvd.
Milwaukee, WI 53210-2941
Tel. 414.445.9736
Fax 414.444.7319
Email: jacpeace@earthlink.net

MARILYN HILL HARPER
1301 Clay Street #3
San Francisco, CA 94109
Tel. 415.771.3722
Fax 415.928.4971
Email:
marilynhh@earthlink.net

BJ GALLAGHER HATELEY
Peacock Productions
701 Danforth Drive
Los Angeles, CA 90065
Tel. 213.227.6205
Fax 213.227.0705
Email: peacockhq@aol.com

GARY W. JANKA
1326 San Migeul Ave.
Santa Barbara, CA 93109
Tel. 805.966.2477
Fax 805.962.1562
Email: gwjanka@silcom.com

SYLVIA LAFAIR
Creative Energy Options
PO Box 87
Will Haven, PA 19477
Tel. 570.636.3858 or
505.471.3542
Email: ceoinc@msn.com

NORMAN LEAR
Act III Productions
100 North Crescent Dr. #250
Beverly Hills, CA 90210
Tel. 310.385.4111
Fax 310.385.4011

WENDY NOMATHEMBA LUHABE
Bridging the Gap
PO Box 91413
Auckland Park 2006
South Africa
Tel. 27.11.482.4840 x3
Fax 27.11.482.5099
Email: wluhab@global.co.za

JOHN R. O'NEIL
The Center for Leadership
    Renewal
PO Box 29491, The Presidio
San Francisco, CA 94129-
Tel. 415.561.6557
Fax 415.561.6465
Email: jroneil@earthlink.net

PATRICK O'NEILL
Extraordinary
    Conversations Inc.
74 The Esplanade
Toronto, Ontario M6S 2W1
Canada
Tel. 416.361.3331
Fax 416.361.3284
Email:
patrick@extraordinary.on.ca

PERVIZ E. RANDERIA
40 Lupine Ave.
San Francisco, CA 94118
Tel. 415.386.6318
Fax 415.751.7049
Email: pervera@aol.com

JOHN RENESCH
PO Box 472379
San Francisco, CA 94147
Tel. 415.437.6974
Fax 415.474.7202
Email: john@renesch.com

WARREN H. SCHMIDT
Chrysalis, Inc.
9238 Petit Ave.
Sepulveda, CA 91343
Tel. 818.892.3092
Fax 818.892.6991
Email: wschmidt@ucla.edu

MICHAEL G. WELP
EqualVoice
3612 46th Avenue South
Minneapolis, MN 55406
Tel. 612.722.7610
Fax 612.722.3910
Email: michael@equalvoice.com
Web: www.equalvoice.com,
www.WhiteMenAndDiversity.com

SUZIE WILLIAMS
8 Glenleigh Dr.
Little Rock, AR 72227
Tel. 501.221.7226
Fax 501.228.2007
Email: swdcw@swbell.net

Index